I0160470

God's Winners' Circle

(Understanding Your Personal Relationship With God)

George Constantine

God's Winners' Circle (Understanding Your Personal Relationship With God)

God's Winners' Circle (Understanding Your Personal Relationship With God)

The contents of this book is intended to be informational only, and based on Christian principles on the practice of faith in God. It is meant to be educational and to complement, and not intended to replace consultations from qualified Christian clergy.

Copyright © 2016 George Constantine, All rights reserved

ISBN-13: 978-0-9917237-2-0 (Spiritual Freedom Publishing)
ISBN-10: 0991723724

Thirsting to find you Lord....

Contents

Contents

Preface

Before all else, this book is dedicated to you who are running the good race of faith. You are bound by a common bond: you seek a spiritual relationship with God, and are in hot pursuit of the highest spiritual expression: to set firm spiritual roots alongside Him in His circle...God's Winners' Circle.

(By the way, all credit deservedly belongs to the Lord, the driving-force that encouraged the creation of this book...)

What you are about to read is a two-part result of a thirty-year journey; the first part is about discovering something incredibly life-changing about yourself...and how it has been kept away from your awareness; the second part is about unleashing this incredible discovery to improve your life and your relationship with God.

At this stage of your faith-journey, you are likely at a level of faith where either you:

a) are just beginning to explore your faith in God, or:
b) are looking deeper into Jesus' message, or:
c) are already living the message of Christ-freedom in your daily
   life and want to take it higher, or:
d) joined a church (or already a member, or thinking about it), or:
e) trying to get in-touch with God...

You want to be closer to God in a personal way where He is involved in every part your life, every step of the way...

You want to be firmly planted in God's Winners' Circle!

You want your heart to shine with immeasurable joy in every good thing that you do, and to share that joy with The Lord...

But there may be a few snags blocking your way...

Have you ever wondered why good things don't happen more often in your life? Or you don't feel as connected to God as you want to be? Or your mind cannot get a full knowledge of how to get close to Him, even though you believe and are actively searching for Him?

The time has come to remove the blockage; you are about to experience your next revelation that will release the power of God's Word in your life:

1. of who you really are to God and to the world around you;
2. understanding what is really holding you back from a wonderful spiritual experience, and:
3. how to get close and personal to God like never before...

It's a new opportunity to skyrocket you to an outstanding relationship with the Lord, restoring your excitement for real spiritual interaction, freely and voluntarily!

You will immediately sense the shift, like a mental block suddenly lifting away; it will ignite a growing excitement in you as you sense a mysterious inner understanding taking hold. You will draw closer to God and you will see wonderful changes occurring in your life as you settle into God's Winners' Circle...and you will want more!

A NEW REVELATION ABOUT THE ENEMY

Deep within the caverns of his dark universe, The Enemy (ie. Satan, sometimes called The Deceiver, The Destroyer, The Devil, The Prince of Darkness, etc...) has kept a collection of secret spiritual weapons from view, hidden away in the shadows and away from your full understanding. They are his darlings, the core from which all his secret operations have been launched against humanity since the beginning of time; and he intends to keep using them to keep you away from having a close and active relationship with the Lord.

You are already aware of his dark spiritual presence that "prowls around like a roaring lion looking for someone to devour (1 Peter 5:8)." The Enemy's mission is to divide and conquer your heart, mind, and soul away from Lord God.

It brings to mind that many brothers and sisters in Christ are aware of the various spiritual tools that can be used to drive back The Enemy's offensive: prayer, fasting, love, God's Word in the Bible, and of course Jesus...yet a great many folks out there fail to experience the full relationship benefit of salvation-joy and the blessings promised by the Lord; sometimes, they receive the blessings and favor, sometimes not.

Why is that?

In spite of the answers available in the Bible (and you may know them very well), you are still vulnerable to spiritual separation because:

1. you do not understand who you really are to God;
2. you have not yet understood the obscured and closely guarded weapons that Satan uses to suppress you.

iii

It makes you subject to a distorted mindset which renders God's Word ineffective in your natural and spiritual life...

This book is really about YOU: to understand the tremendous potential that has been implanted within youself, a potential that has been limited by The Enemy's interference in your life...

It is also meant to inspire you to understand how to break-out of your spiritual oppression, and expose the "spiritual blockers" that interfere with your personal relationship with God...

You will then be introduced to an effective way to understand your own built-in potential to reach out, and get closer to God. In fact, you will discover that God had already set the stage for your reconciliation with Him, and this will really get you excited!

It will encourage you to reflect upon what you are about to read, and how it can affect your own life and faith. It is meant to stir a different way of thinking, a new understanding of how to trigger more of God's power in your own journey...

You will break through your barriers, and reach a higher spiritual understanding with this extraordinary revelation. It will only make the Good News Message from Christ so much more exciting and in-focus for you to enjoy and build upon!

PART ONE: THE PROBLEM

Introduction

"Removing The Scales"

"And immediately something like scales fell from his eyes, and he regained his sight...(Acts 9:18, ESV)"

It is not every day that you come to discover something that can change your life in an instant...a missing link that opens up the floodgates to new heights and possibilities...an eye-opener!

Today is one such moment; your time has arrived for a major discovery...and a new level of spiritual revival!

Get ready to make your most important breakthrough in your faith...the greatest ever!

You are about to embark on a journey that will be very personal, and it will demand some reflection, especially if you have wondered how to get into a deeper personal relationship with God.

Have you ever had a personal goal? It was a goal that you wanted bad enough, and willing to work hard to get it...regardless of the obstacles and difficulties ahead (examples: aiming for a dream career; as a student wanting top grades; as a doctor doing the greatest job possible for his patients; a teacher wanting to be the best mentor for his/her students; the ideal secretary; the business owner wanting to expand his business; build a new porch; buy a new house; renovate the kitchen...etc.)?

Reaching out and rising higher in your spiritual goals is no different: you need to work at it, repositioning yourself into a *new level of understanding* the real importance of yourself, your world, and your real relationship with God; at the same time you will understand how The Enemy, Satan (sometimes called The Deceiver, The Destroyer, The Complicator...), is actually interfering and preventing your full fellowship with God, depriving you of the blessings and favor that were intended for you since the day you were born.

You are about to come face-to-face with an obscured truth: who and what you really are, and why the devil wants it obscured from your awareness. It is cloaked and hidden from your full understanding by an equally obscured, and closely-guarded set of weapons that Satan uses against you; they are the most sinister weapons of all time and a major spiritual obstacle to your spiritual rebirth and restoration.

They've been used over and over again throughout the ages, and with a great deal of success because they are purposely kept obscured; at the same time they are staring right at you but you don't see them, and that's the genius behind Satan and his secret weapons...

Once you realize what they are, you can neutralize The Enemy's ability to affect your life, your relationship with God and His Champion of Freedom, Jesus.

Here's what you are about to discover:

vi

1) Your own secret weapon (born with it and never knew about it);
2) The real weapons behind Satan's power (it's not what you think);
3) How Satan manipulates your own secret weapon against you;
4) God's Winners' Circle, and how you can be part of it.

Understanding The Surgical Strike Against You

The spiritual war against humanity has spiraled out of control in these last days, cutting-off so many from God, and it will continue until there is no one left to save...

As a believing Christian, you are already free and saved through Jesus Christ. But the Enemy isn't giving up; he continues his spiritual terrorism against you and the whole world, with the intention of luring everyone away from the joy and freedom in Christ...back into a joyless, sorrowful life full of complications, unfulfilled goals, psychological enslavement, and negative thinking.

The Enemy Wants Chaos

Satan wants to disrupt and distort your life by:

a) cutting-off your contact with God;
b) cutting-off your peaceful salvation-joy found in Jesus;
c) cutting-off your good relationships, including Christ;
d) cutting-off God's divine intentions for you;

Disruption and distortion are meant to de-sensitize, separate you from being part of God's Winners' Circle.

Satan's Weapons Of Total Chaos

You've heard the term 'weapons of mass destruction' (WMDs) describing nuclear bombs, biological and chemical weapons, with the potential of killing millions...

Well, The Enemy also has his own version of WMDs...and has done more damage to the world than anyone or anything else!

Satan's Weapons of Total Chaos have wreaked havoc since the start, destroying billions of souls over the course of history...and his 'soul-count' is still growing!

The Ultimate Deception...Exposed Right Now

There hasn't been a greater deception in human history (this will really blow you away)...

Understand that:

-lust;
-gluttony;
-sloth;
-pride;
-fear;
-hate;
-anger;
-jealousy;
-envy;
-desire;
-addiction;

-self-pity;
-manipulation;
-self-indulgence;
-confusion;
-cheating;
-lying;
-greed;
-selfishness;
-suspicion;
-intolerance;
-boredom;
-frivolity;
-alcoholism;
-drugs;
-abuse;
-violence...etc...

...are NOT Satan's primary weapons against you (maybe you thought they were).

Truth is, they are all decoys...the **results** of Satan's Weapons Of Total Chaos!

If you thought that your lack of faith or bad experiences in life are caused by hate, jealousy, envy...or any of the above...then **you've been effectively decoyed by Satan!**

Check it out yourself:

Do you blame your bad circumstances on any of the"causes" mentioned above?

Have you been trying to find answers to these so-called "causes" above but the problems remain?

If so, then you have been spending precious time chasing down the wrong answers...

You are curing the symptom, but not the disease...

Meanwhile, the true weapons are working behind the scenes, hidden and undetected; they are actually destroying both the intended joy of your life, and your placement in God's Winners' Circle!

The driving force behind all your problems...physical, practical, spiritual...come from Satan's Weapons Of Total Chaos...

But before revealing them to you, you will be first introduced to an incredible weapon of your own, a powerful weapon you are born with...and probably never fully understood its awesome potential...

Chapter 1

Your Strongest Feature...The Enemy's Main Target

Now pay close attention because this will forever change the way you see yourself:

God has implanted a great gift in you...

In fact, He has implanted this gift to your fathers and forefathers, and beyond!

It is one of your strongest features as a free person, and Satan does not want you to know about it...

Put this into your heart:

"You are born to communicate."

Your ability to communicate is the single, most important quality you have as a human being. Your entire biological existence was made for this purpose, to communicate.

Think about it: beginning from the moment of your birth you are communicating:

As a baby you communicated non-verbally through sounds and

involuntary jestures (crying, looking, smiling, touching) as your mind began to discover the world...

As you grew, you developed skills to express what you had been thinking:

1) Communicating Verbally to:

 i)   your mom and dad;
 ii)   your brothers and sisters;
 iii)   your wife;
 iv)   your husband;
 v)   your parents;
 vi)   your kids;
 vii)   friends/relatives;
 viii)   strangers;
 ix)   business associates;
 x)   co-workers;
 xi)   pets, etc.

2) Communicating Physically through:

body-language (touching, certain stances, gestures...);
facial expressions;
touching;
expressing moods;
the clothes you wear;
emotional gestures (happy, sad, angry...);
sounds (clearing your throat to interrupt a conversation...);
technology via computers, texting, phone...

3) Communicating Mentally:

thinking;
rationalizing;
understanding;
learning;
memorizing:
believing;
creating;
imagining;
observing...

4) Communicating spiritually with God...

Your gift of communications is more than just a tool to contact others; it is actually a journey of development: first, to evolve and mature into an effective communicator in the natural world; second, to take it further and get into a close and personal relationship with God by becoming an effective 'spiritual' communicator.

"A word fitly spoken is like apples of gold in a setting of silver (Proverbs 25:11 ESV)..."

Your ability to communicate is more precious than gold. It can help uplift someone in a time of need: it can compliment, insult, make friends (or enemies), paint an impression of who you are...even if you are the most anti-social person in the world, you are still communicating somehow. Your physical body exists so that you can have the ability to communicate.

So keep this deep within your heart:

"You Are Born To Communicate"

God, the Master Engineer...The Creator, expects you to develop your communication skills; He wants you ultimately use it to reach out to Him with your mind, heart, and your mouth:

"May these words of my mouth and this meditation of my heart be pleasing in your sight, Lord (Psalm 19:14 NIV);" and:

"I am about to open my mouth; my words are on the tip of my tongue. My words come from an upright heart (Job 33:2-3 NIV)..."

The Enemy Infiltrates Your Thoughts

Satan knows about the inner strength in you. He knows that your power of communications will open great opportunities at every level of your life when used properly, including a closer personal relationship with God. This is why it is so important for The Enemy to disrupt your power of communication by first distorting your communications in your daily life, and then cutting off your spiritual communications without you being aware of it!

Meanwhile, to reinforce his disruption of your communications, Satan leads you to incorrectly pursue other ideas that are seemingly good, but can inadvertently decoy you away from a close and personal relationship with God, occupying your mind on issues associated with:

Pride, Hate, Anger, Jealousy, Envy, Desire, Addiction, Self-pity, Manipulation, Self-indulgence, Confusion, Cheating, Lying, Greed,

Selfishness, Suspicion, Intolerance, Self-Image, etc...

As noble as your intentions are to deal with these, remember that the whole objective of your spiritual pursuit is to make close, spiritual contact with God. This is what this book is all about: making contact. As bad as selfish pride, hate, anger, jealousy, etc. are, they are merely decoys whose job is to steer your concentration away from your relationship with God...

Your body, your mind, and your thoughts are your personal communications tools; they will either trigger good or bad communications. Either way, The Enemy will use both the good and the bad to plant inaccuracies, and a sea of other misinformation in order to distort your mindset from thinking in a spiritual way; they may seem reasonable, logical, and sensible, but will not generate the kind of personal communication relationship with God.

Rampage of Disconnection

Satan is on a 'disconnection-rampage,' aiming to cause a total disruption of your communications with God, and is targeting his rage on God's favorites: YOU, and the rest of humanity...he's been doing this for a very long time and an expert in his field...

Once you are cut off from God, he will keep you running in circles for a lifetime, complicating your life, placing obstacles in your way, and effectively "jamming your communications!"

Sad to say, it seems that his strategy is working very well. Just look around: global chaos chiseling-away at an unsuspecting world that uses its gift of communications poorly...

Know Your Strength

Before setting your "spiritual bar" higher by diving into "Bible scripture overload," understand the importance of the greatest gift that God has ever given you: your powerful gift of communication. You are a communications powerhouse in a verbal, physical, mental, spiritual way...and Satan wants to sabotage it!

You may have taken your ability to communicate for granted...it's "just something that you do everyday..."

Don't do that...your ability to communicate is far, far more important!

Re-align your understanding of God's plan for you and for your future generations: understand the importance of your power to communicate! It should make more sense now: it isn't only about communicating good things about yourself, about others, about your job tasks, etc; ultimately, it's all about reaching out to God.

Do you sense an urgency rising up in you, a new desire to learn more about the power of your own communication? Do you want to understand how Satan can inflict your disconnection from God, replacing it with communications chaos? Your choice can have far-reaching effects in both your personal, public, and spiritual communications life.

You are now ready for your next revelation: to learn about Satan's Weapons Of Total Chaos that were briefly mentioned in the Introduction. Once you understand their intentions, you can disable Satan's ability to keep you permanently disconnected from the goodness of this world and your personal relationship with God in God's Winners' Circle...

Chapter 2

First Weapon: The Beginnings of a Life Destroyed

You will now be introduced to the first of Satan's Weapons of Total Chaos (SWTC).

Billions of people are needless victims of this terrible weapon...

Introducing: IGNORANCE.

You're probably saying, "That's it? Isn't it more sophisticated than that?"

Understand this:

"There is a kind of sophistication going on here that goes beyond any human invention, and vastly more complex than computers, satellites, and so on..."

Ignorance is one of them.

"Well I already know what it is to be ignorant," you might say...

But do you?

There are plenty of levels of Ignorance...but the greatest Ignorance above all else are these:

a) Not knowing you are created for communication;
b) Ignorance is a major component creating a gap between you and your personal relationship with God...

Within this context, Ignorance becomes a very serious issue; Jesus and his disciples talked about it:

"You are mistaken, not understanding the Scriptures nor the power of God (Matthew 22:29, New American Standard)..." and:

"Therefore having overlooked the times of ignorance, God is now declaring to men that all people everywhere should repent...(Acts 17:29-30)..."

Satan Wants You Cut-Off From God

God has implanted in you the ability to communicate both with your world, and most importantly with Him. The Enemy knows this, and has a supernatural agenda to have you cut-off from God by any means possible; what better way to do it than by sabotaging your knowledge of this incredible ability to communicate!

Now picture this: disruption of communication infecting everyone on a global scale...with The Enemy at the helm wreaking havoc all over the world since the beginning of time...

The warnings are plenty, but here's one warning as written in the Bible:

"Be alert and of sober mind. Your enemy the devil prowls around like a roaring lion looking for someone to devour (1 Peter 5:8, NIV)..."

Suddenly all the wars, the genocides, the murders, domestic disputes, the subtle misunderstandings, the kidnappings, the rapes, bad attitudes, etc. make sense: all caused largely due to Ignorance of the awesome importance of mankind's ultimate purpose: communication with your world and with God!

Ignorance: A Dubious Stage

You were ignorant the moment you were born, but you didn't stay that way; you began to learn about yourself, about life; and you continued to learn and have become wiser. So Ignorance in itself is not evil; everyone starts out that way, but you don't stay that way: your life-journey is meant to make you wiser through learning and personal interaction (communication) with your world. Eventually you discover that your interactions are not limited only to the natural world, but can transcend into the spiritual...

And this is not what The Enemy wants! With Ignorance, he keeps you away from *specific* knowledge essential to your personal development, such as your powerful potential to develop your communication at the highest level as a person of excellence within your world, and God's!

So as an eye-opener, think on this: you can be a devout Christian, and yet be cut off from God without knowing it because you:

1) Were kept from knowing this great power within you, or:
2) Have not fully understood your power of communication.

Ignorance can set-up your lifelong-journey without fulfilling your inner desire for personal communications contact with God. It is a process that progressively takes you off-course discreetly. It is in fact a battle that cannot be won single-handedly because:

The Deceiver can set the disconnection-stage against you before you were born: the Ignorance of your forefathers...

    a) He uses time, destroying your entire family-line for generations;
    b) Will apply Ignorance through good and bad circumstances (to draw your communications away from God).

Make no mistake: The Enemy uses all the circumstances available to sabotage your spiritual mindset away from God; Ignorance is one of his key resources against you...

Modern Times Can Be Tough

In today's modern world where humanity is enjoying its highest level of quality of life, the Enemy can easily keep you away from contact with God by using various modern communication conveniences:

-The world of television, video games, working long hours, debt, stress, clubs, drugs, etc;
-The glitter of the material world making you desire more of the physical, not the spiritual...

It can make you believe that communicating with God is 'old-fashioned thinking', not fitting in today's modern, fast-track world:

"...their thinking became futile and their foolish hearts were darkened. Although they claimed to be wise, they became fools and exchanged the glory of the immortal God (Romans 1:21-23 NIV)..."

(Note: modern day technology, creativity, and progress is not a bad thing...they are another of God's great gifts for you to enjoy and interact with...they are part of your learning curve that is supposed to lead you toward your ultimate experience, which is enjoyment and greatful interaction with God)

If you are not aware of the true nature behind Ignorance (keeping you from understanding the true importance of your gift of communications, and that Ignorance is a major component in Satan's arsenal against you), then you are open to spiritual separation coming in the form of:

pride,
hate,
anger,
jealousy,
envy,
want,
addiction,
self-pity,
manipulation,
self-indulgence,
complications,
finances,
marriage problems...etc...

...with each one designed to bog you down into the "fog of life" and distancing your understanding of how your own built-in communications can restore supernatural contact with God.

Checklist To Determine If You Are Aware Of Ignorance

1) Were you ever aware that you are a person born to communicate?
2) You are alive so that you can communicate?
3) That Ignorance can separate you from God?
4) That it prevents development of personal interaction with God?

If your answer is "no" to any of the above, then you are a victim of Satan's Weapons Of Total Chaos, through his first weapon, Ignorance.

Remember: even though you may have accepted Jesus into your life, you still need to 'run the good race of faith' and celebrate your salvation-joy victory by sharing your joy with God. As a follower of Christ, you know The Deceiver is trying to PREVENT you from celebrating your salvation, prowling around "like a roaring lion looking for someone to devour (1 Peter 5:8, NIV)."

This is what Satan is 'prowling' for: Christians and non-Christians who have left themselves vulnerable to Ignorance.

And the greatest Ignorance: not knowing that you are a person born to communicate...and this leads to separation from God.

Chapter 3

Second Weapon

Satan absolutely loves the next secret weapon because no one takes notice of it...and his success against you depends on it.

It is called LAZINESS.

"Oh no, another lame weapon! Satan has no sophisticated weapons!" you might say.

Realize that Laziness is a very sophisticated weapon...AND IT WORKS! By trivializing the destructive power of Laziness, you are falling into the trap of Ignorance (too lazy to find out keeps you ignorant...see how they work together?)!

Remember that The Enemy's secret weapons are completely different than lasers, machine-guns, and cruise missiles...he uses BETTER weapons that can slip right under your radar and ultimately disrupt your contact with God!

Laziness is one of his choice weapons...

Getting Lazy in Small Doses

Satan is not particularly interested in exposing his intentions against you; his actions are subtle, making you spiritually lazy little-by-little...

As with Ignorance, The Enemy will use your natural vulnerabilities to slowly fall into a lazy state of mind about spiritual matters by:

1. not actively developing your gift of communication, making you believe re-contact with God is hard, so why bother?
2. believing that you need to spend too much energy for supernatural intervention in your busy life;
3. being unmotivated to take on the effort of spiritual revival due to the burdens of everyday life;
4. other "more important things" to take care of...you'll get spiritual later...

Does any of the above seem familiar to you?

Satan's ultimate goal is to get you lazy enough in mind and body so that any effort to get close to God would be "too much" or "you don't feel like doing it." He will make the easy and uncomplicated Good News Message look as if it would take an excess amount of motivation to read (even though it's the easiest).

Along with Ignorance, The Enemy will try to frustrate any of your attempts to establish and maintain a spiritual communication-link with God; he can, and oftentimes will, discourage your genuine interest to the point where Laziness can creep into your mindset...

You've seen it happen in everyday life: For example, you need to cut the grass, but you decide you'll do it later (two weeks go by and the grass almost stands taller than you...just joking!); the dishes need cleaning, but you leave it until the next day when the dirty dishes are stacked all over the counter; the room needs to be painted...that was a year ago; you are going to stop taking drugs, or keen on working hard to getting your school grades up, or joining a gym to lose some weight...but you never took action.

At first, your excitement for a personal relationship with God may be genuine; but it didn't go any further than just some good-willed intention that never materializes. Laziness slowly drifts into your mind, convincing you that any effort to re-establish a close and personal relationship with God can wait...especially when you have other priorities in your life...

Your God-given gift of communications becomes a part-time concern. You become so drained from life itself that you'd be playing "catch-up" with your faith...and many folks out there find this discouraging, too much work. You end up falling into a lazy state of mind; your ability to communicate with God becomes something "to do later."

And The Enemy is not stupid; he knows human nature! He knows that you can get yourself back on-track with the enabling power of the Word in the Bible; but he also knows that the Word can be rendered ineffective if your mind finds it tiresome, especially when you convince yourself that you are burdened with life's challenges and have no time for spiritual matters.

Too Much Effort

The word "Laziness" should no longer be in your vocabulary

because it is an energy-drainer, both spiritually and physically...look how the Bible describes it:

"Laziness brings deep sleep, and the shiftless go hungry (Proverbs 19:15 NIV), and:

"Diligent hands will rule, but laziness ends in forced labor (Proverbs 12:24 NIV)...

Laziness always finds a way to discourage positive action by infecting your thinking.

You find "reasonable excuses" like:

a) not enough time;
b) you are tired;
c) have other priorities;
d) stressed-out; depressed, discouraged;
e) 'not really into it,' etc.

Laziness creeps into your mind even if you DO believe in God and are a practicing Christian! Some of the faithful will even resort to forcefully pray to God on specific time schedules because they feel an obligation to pray, even while the mind is lazily drifting from one thought to another.

Jesus spoke of this in parable of the sower of seeds in Luke 8:

"A sower went out to sow his seed (Luke 8:5)...And some fell on the rock, and as it grew up it withered away because it had no moisture. And some fell among the thorns, and the thorns grew up with it and choked it (Luke 8:7-8, ESV)..."

16

He then explained:

"And the ones on the rock are those who, when they hear the word, receive it with joy. But these have no root; they believe for a while, and in time of testing fall away. And as for what fell among the thorns, they are those who hear, but as they go on their way they are choked by the cares and riches and pleasures of life, and their fruit does not mature (Luke 8:13-14 ESV)..."

Satan uses the cares, worries, and pleasures of this life to encourage Laziness by feeding your mind energy-draining ideas such as:

"Relax! The Word takes too much out of you...go watch some television and get your mind off things...play some video games...go fix the shed...paint a room...clean the kitchen...you've got time to talk to Him later on...God understands."

While it is true that God understands your daily burdens, your intention of 'getting back to God later on' sometimes never comes; you slowly drift away, thinking you can get back to God, but you don't, at least not with the same enthusiasm...

In other words you get lazy, even to communicate with God. This loss of enthusiasm sets the stage for powerless spiritual communications, preventing any close and personal relationship with God to ever develop:

"We do not want you to become lazy, but to imitate those who through faith and patience inherit what has been promised...(Hebrews 6:12 NIV)..."

It Does Not Stop There

Laziness not only affects your faith; it also infiltrates every stage of your life.

This includes:

i)   affecting your own proper upbringing as a child;
ii) infiltrating your relationships;
iii) interfering with natural/spiritual nurturing of your children;
iv) invading your life activities (work, play, etc...);
v)   changing your character;
vi) altering your thinking...

Understand the significance of Laziness: it's ok to be lazy at times and not do anything...it can be therapeudic! But in the spiritual sense, look at its association with Ignorance because together they give birth to The Enemy's next weapon...perhaps the coldest weapon of all-time...

Chapter 4

Third Weapon

Ever heard someone say they are:

a) 'numb to the world';
b) disconnected;
c) don't care;
d) not excited about anything;
e) not interested in anything;
f) a meaningless life;
g) not attracted to anything emotional...etc?

These are but a small group of expressions describing the next weapon used against you by The Enemy:

INDIFFERENCE

It means losing passion and excitement about something, a total disconnection...an "I don't care" attitude.

When your heart and mind become Indifferent to God, you are no longer interested in spending the time or energy toward Him...

You become disconnected from Him...you don't even feel like communicating with God, or anyone else for that matter:

"But they refused to pay attention; stubbornly they turned their backs and covered their ears. They made their hearts as hard as flint and would not listen to the law or to the words that the Lord Almighty had sent by His Spirit through the earlier prophets...(Zechariah 7:11-12 NIV)..."

Your Life Turned Out Differently

Sometimes you are indifferent because things haven't gone your way: "Well God doesn't seem to care about me, so why should I care about Him?" or: "Everyone is out for themselves, dog-eat-dog, so I won't care about anyone else but me..."

Remember that Satan's goal is to separate you from God in any way possible...and he will start by draining (or preventing you from ever discovering) your spiritual side through tough circumstances in your daily life, with Ignorance and Laziness helping along the way...

Eventually you get fed up with everything and fall into Indifference.

That's Only The Beginning

Chapter 1 (Your Strongest Feature) revealed that you are born to communicate. Your biological existence was purposely built for communication; it is your greatest strength as a physical/spiritual person. God wants you to nurture and develop your communications ability so that you can reach out to Him with meaningful, loving communication.

Understand that God wants to hear from you. He's expecting you to 'tune-in' to Him...but imagine what happens when you fall into Indifference?

You simply stop caring about being with Him; you may no longer be interested. In fact, Indifference can make you stop caring about plenty of things if you are not careful:

your wife,
your kids,
your friends,
your job,
your circumstances,
your destiny,
your interests,
your world,
your communication with God,
your intended (and promised) blessings and miracles in your life...

Everything is affected as you fall into a negative mindset, with the terrible possibility of never finding your way back into a spiritually meaningful life with God, and the joyous feeling of being saved in Christ...all because you don't care:

"The person without the Spirit does not accept the things that come from the Spirit of God but considers them foolishness, and cannot understand them because they are discerned only through the Spirit (Corinthians 2:14 NIV)," and:

"When I called, they did not listen (Zechariah 7:13)..."

Zest For Life Removed

Along with Ignorance and Laziness, Indifference kills the zest-for-life...

"But life is tough, and I'm not getting what I expected of it, so I've become cold and skeptical," you may be thinking.

You resort to finding excitement in superficial things, 'feel-good' addictions because they give you a false sense of meaning, and can lead to seriously bad decisions, and not even caring about who you hurt (examples):

i)   Infidelity;
ii) Abusive attitude to others and yourself;
iii) Selfish; Impatient;
iv) Substance/material abuser (drugs, alcohol, compulsive buyer...);
v) Overly materialistic (cars, jewelry, big house, etc)...

The Enemy loves to develop Indifference in your heart, and uses it constantly on the things that are important to you: failed dreams, lost relationships, etc. He nurtures Indifference by first nurturing your Ignorance and Laziness. Equally important to him is the spiritual effect of Indifference: removing any passion and desire to stay tuned-in to God.

Indifference will affect your natural life by increasing your apathy, hate, intolerance to everything (example: your job, the endless bills, stress in your relationships, problems with your kids, not enough 'alone time'...etc):

"What causes fights and quarrels among you? Don't they come from your desires that battle within you? You desire but do not have, so you kill. You covet but you cannot get what you want, so you quarrel and fight...When you ask, you do not receive because you ask with wrong motives, that you may spend what you get on your pleasures (James 4:1-3, NIV)."

Sometimes things don't happen the way you'd expect; they bring along circumstances that can frustrate your life. Certain circumstances can even become potential 'spiritual-blockers' that can interfere with your spiritual journey; they can discourage your communications with God, and feed your Indifference to the powerful potential of God's promises in your life.

When Indifference strikes, it sets up the last stage of Satan's Weapons of Total Chaos...his "cherry on the top" that completes the total breakdown of communication with God...

Chapter 5

Fourth Weapon

Heard of the expression "Out of Sight, Out of Mind?"

There is another word that describes the same thing. It is called:

FORGETFULNESS.

Being forgetful is normal...everyone forgets something! But the kind of forgetting here goes far deeper than just 'forgetting the car keys on the counter!' It's about forgetting the one single component that can start you on the path to a personal relationship with the Lord in God's Winners' Circle:

Forgetting about your important gift of communication!

Your gift of communication is an invitation from God to reach out and interact with Him; no other creation has the ability to do so: no plant, no rock, no insect...

And it does not stop there; with Forgetfulness, you don't remember:

i)   how important you are as one born to communicate;
ii)   Ignorance, Laziness, Indifference (and Forgetfulness);
iii)   the life-altering power of your relationship with God;
iv)   your free communications with God;
v)   your appreciation of Him;
vi)   your mindfulness Him;
vii)   that He can help you in your everyday life;
viii) favor and blessings are possible when tuned-in with God;
ix)   supernatural salvation is within your reach;
x)   His Champion Jesus and what He did (and can do) for you...

A Cruel Weapon Too Often Used

Just like the other three (Ignorance, Laziness, Indifference),
Forgetfulness can affect the practical part of your life such as:

-Personal goals;
-The sacredness of your marriage;
-Your proper nurturing of your children;
-Taking care of yourself;
-Considering the well-being of others;
-Your community;
-The beauty of life;
-Your self-confidence;
-Respecting others;
-Your attitude;
-Your joy...

And usually you put the blame of your forgetfulness on some
excuse:

a) another person;

b) some circumstance;

c) bad luck;

d) too busy;

e) doesn't "fit your schedule;"

f) not interested...

The cruel reality behind Forgetfulness is that it affects your ability to communicate: it is reduced to the point that you even *forget* how important communication is in your life; forgetting WHY you are given this ability to communicate in the first place (to ultimately understand and reach out to God, and to never forget):

"The covenant that I have made with you, you shall not forget...(2 Kings 17:38 NAS)"

Satan Loves You, Sort-of...

Shocking isn't it? The devil wants you to live a full and rewarding life...but without God. With all the pleasures and worries of the world at your possession, The Enemy can easily get you to forget God!

He executes his plan of Ignorance, Laziness, and Indifference so that God becomes your last priority...and then tops it off by making you Forget God's importance in your everyday life...

You might still be a casual believer in God; but "casual belief" is enough for The Destroyer to get a firm foothold and start you on the road of total spiritual disconnection through Forgetfulness....

Satan Fills Your Void

To replace God in your life, The Enemy will make sure that Forgetfulness will steer your mind into ideologies, philosophies, and "feel-good" ways of life that will cut off your contact to God; he will use:

a) the good (a rewarding career, a nice family life-style, active in your community, world-traveller, self-made millionaire, popular, busy, etc.), and:

b) the bad (debt-ridden, unhappy, unfulfilled, unscrupulous, miserly, bad attitude, etc.)...

Yes, *even good events in your life* can be used toward the same goal: tuning-out your communications with God by Forgetting.

It might seem all innocent to you: you are simply following the ways of the world, reaching out to all the beautiful things it has to offer, sometimes with good results, sometimes bad...and you forget God.

God expects you to live a progressive life that can become a rewarding experience overall; still, the very same 'razzle-dazzle' can equally lure you away from the Lord if you are not careful:

"When you have eaten and are satisfied, you shall bless the Lord your God for the good land which He has given you. Beware that you do not forget your God...otherwise, when you have eaten and are satisfied...then your heart will become proud and you will forget the Lord your God...(Deuteronomy 8:10-14 NAS)."

And that's what The Enemy wants to do: with Forgetfulness, his primary task is to lead you astray from the Lord.

The enemy's goal:

- Forget God...
- Forget Christ...
- Forget Ignorance, Laziness, Indifference...
- Forget spiritual maturity...
- Forget Harmony and Salvation-Joy...
- Forget your power of communication...
- Forget Forgetfulness!

Chapter 6

Second Wave...You Thought Was The First

Once the first wave has distorted your communications with God (with Ignorance, Laziness, Indifference, Forgetfullness), The Enemy then proceeds with his second wave of assault against you.

The second wave works hand-in-hand with the first, and insures separation between you and God. They are:

Temptation, Distraction, Complication.

"Aha! I know those!" you might say.

But here is where your mindset has fallen victim to the REAL DECEPTION:

Until today, you may had considered Temptation-Distraction-Complication as Satan's PRIMARY weapons against you (just as plenty of folks thought the same about pride, selfishness, anger, hate, lying, jealousy, etc.); you probably thought they were the real causes to your daily challenges...

You now realize this is not so.

Temptation-Distraction-Complication are the **second-wave of attack**, and they are dead-on effective once Ignorance, Laziness, Indifference, and Forgetfulness have begun your downward spiral...

As your mindset is weakened by Satan's Weapons Of Total Chaos, you can then be "Tempted to be Distracted into some kind of Complication..."

...and you are cut off from God.

Temptation

The Enemy absolutely enjoys using Temptation once your mind and thinking have been distorted in Ignorance-Laziness-Indifference-Forgetfulness...

Everywhere you look there are tempting circumstances that can lead you in making decisions in every part of your life, be it private, public, financial, physical, good, bad, spiritual...anything that has the potential to keep you separated from God.

Even Jesus went through a period of temptation:

"...Jesus was led by the Spirit into the wilderness to be tempted (Matthew 4:1-11)."

Have you ever been tempted by anything in your lifetime? Was it buying a bigger house you can't afford; the more expensive car, a prestigious watch, arrogant or hateful of others who are more successful than you; discouragement because life hasn't turned out your way; falling into self-pity; that extra piece of apple pie around midnight while trying to lose weight...etc?

Temptation can lead to both desirable and undesirable consequences, but its ultimate goal is always the same: to pull you away from your contact with God.

The Enemy knows your weaknesses, and will use Temptation to lure you away from your spiritual goals.

Look at the process:

1) Satan will first use his Weapons of Total Chaos (Ignorance Laziness-Indifference-Forgetfulness) to set up your mind (your 'mindset') for spiritual disconnection, alter your thinking to limit your gift of communications...

2) Deepen the divide between yourself, your world and God by tempting circumstances...in the form of thought-temptations, word temptations, and deed-temptations.

3) Your failure is imminent as temptations in your thoughts, words, and deeds can distract you away from God, God's Word, and His Messenger: Jesus...

4) The ultimate result: you are deprived of your personal spiritual connection that brings supernatural blessings, and your miraculous salvation in Christ.

Distraction

Once Temptation has lured your attention into the open and away from the spiritual, Distraction continues the campaign of your disconnection by feeding you constant diversions in your life.

During his testing in the desert, Jesus was presented with various distractions in order to tempt Him:

"...the tempter came to him and said, "If you are the Son of God, tell these stones to become bread..." (Matt 4:4 NIV)..."

"Again, the devil took him to a very high mountain and showed him all the kingdoms of the world and their splendor. "All this I will give you" he said, "if you will bow down and worship me..." (Matthew 4:8 NIV)."

Even Jesus was tempted to be distracted with something as great as being offered the whole world...sometimes a good thing is not always the best thing! The point here is that distractions can divert (and deceive) even the most spiritually dedicated...no one is immune. If you are not careful to maintain your communication-link with God, then you can be assured that Satan will use any distraction to wear you down and cut you off...and there are plenty of Distractions out there, too many actually...!

Distraction can even make you think that:

You still believe in God;
You worship Him and love Him;
You may be on His side...

But your connection to Him is cut, **and may not even know it!**

You may be distracted even at this very moment (example: reading this, but you can hear the news on t.v. in the backround...)!

There are plenty of warnings about the dangers of distraction in the Bible:

"...Ponder the path of your feet; then all your ways will be sure...(Proverbs 4:25-27)..." and:

"...Mary, who sat at the Lord's feet and listened to his teaching. But Martha was distracted...Martha, Martha, you are anxious and troubled about many things (Luke 10:39-41)," etc...

Distraction is definitely part of The Enemy's second wave of attack against you and your communication effectiveness with God.

Complication

Human ambition can produce some extraordinary results when channelled properly...but The Deceiver loves to transform them into the kinds of complications that can potentially cut you off from your relationship with God.

But here's something you probably did not know:

His objective isn't necessarily to completely destroy you...The Enemy wants to keep you around!

Surprised?

You shouldn't be!

Satan wants you to be his trophy...a living spiritual failure to be triumphantly displayed to God, discouraging others seeking salvation!

As long as you remain out-of-contact from God (the result of Ignorance-Laziness-Indifference-Forgetfulness), you belong to The Enemy. He can throw you off your spiritual journey by complicating your life with good and bad circumstances (bad marriage, overwhelming bills, working toward success, rich, hurt pride, hateful, envious, a perfect busy life, lack of confidence, infidelity, anxiety, "fed-up with your problems," etc), while you struggle to maintain your spirituality:

"Anxiety weighs down the heart (Proverbs 12:25)..."

Satan's hope is that you will also infect others in your disconnected state as you spiral them away from the Lord.

And how can you infect those around you?

By keeping God out of the picture entirely! The complications in your life may not come in the natural sense; it could also be spiritual.

Progressive Separation From God

The Enemy is so clever...

He knows that you are on guard and trying your best to stay in-contact with the Lord...

But The Deceiver is patient, and will use:

i) time, weakening your faith and cutting off contact with God;
ii) circumstances, good or bad, stripping your trust in God;

iii) your lack of preparedness against Ignorance, Laziness, Indifference, Forgetfullness;

iv) not using the supernatural power of the Word, and Christ who shows you how to use it...

He will use Temptations, Distractions, and Complications to divert your focus from well-intentioned activities such as:

Career,
Family,
Ambition,
Prosperity,
Success,
Helping the community,
Excellence in leadership,
Wholesome entertainment,
Well-Being,
Joy,
Pride,
Self-esteem,
Confidence, etc...and transforming them into something distorted, negative:

Career Overload,
Neglected Family Values,
Selfish Ambition,
Miserly,
Egotistical,
Greedy,
Self-Indulgent,
Self-Interested,
Self-Centered...etc:

"For people will be lovers of self, lovers of money, proud, arrogant, abusive, disobedient to their parents, ungrateful, unholy, heartless, unappeasable, slanderous, without self-control, brutal, not loving good, treacherous, reckless, swollen with conceit, lovers of pleasure rather than lovers of God, having the appearance of godliness, but denying its power (2 Timothy 3 ESV)..."

It brings less reliance in God, more devotion to yourself, even blaming God for any problems that may rise...no gratitude to God, only a selfish never-ending appetite to fulfill some inner desire...

And then you wonder why your life seems dull, and not going your way; or you may have become successful but you have been neglecting those who love you...even indulging into activities that may be disastrous (paying less attention to your family, having an affair, drug or alcohol abuse, growing disinterest in everything other than yourself...etc).

The deception becomes all the more clear: The Enemy will use all the available resources (the good and bad) to keep you away from your personal relationship with God:

"For we do not wrestle against flesh and blood, but against the rulers, against the authorities, against the cosmic power over this present darkness, against spiritual forces of evil (Ephesians 6:11-12 ESV)..."

Satan's Helpers

More important is WHO The Enemy is using to weaken you:

You guessed it: OTHER HUMAN BEINGS!

Your greatest asset is your full understanding that you are born to communicate; Satan will manipulate other people's lack of understanding of this very one quality to destroy your contact with God. By using other peoples' Ignorance-Laziness-Indifference-Forgetfulness to influence you away from the Lord, he will set you up for instant disconnection.

You will then be kept that way by using Temptations-Distractions-Complications that come from others around you.

It does NOT mean that your friends and acquaintances are bad people, no. It could mean that:

i) they may be cut off from God and Jesus too;
ii) victims of Satan's scheme (and not knowing it);
iii) have fallen to their own blend of Temptations-Distraction and Complications:

"My people have become lost sheep; their sheperds have led them astray. They have made them turn aside on the mountains (Jeremiah 50:6 NAS)..."

You may be concentrating so much on your own inner efforts to improve yourself that you do not pay attention that other people can make you fall out of contact with God, intentionally or unintentionally...

Chapter 7

A Living Cycle Of Destruction

If Satan's plan was plotted step-by-step, it would look like this:

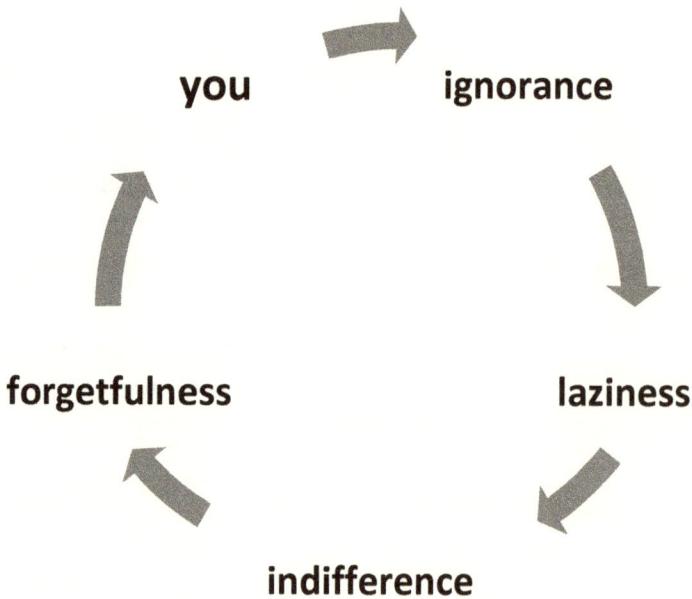

you → **ignorance** → **laziness** → **indifference** → **forgetfulness** → (back to you)

...the first cycle is designed to dominate your mindset;

The second cycle keeps you dominated:

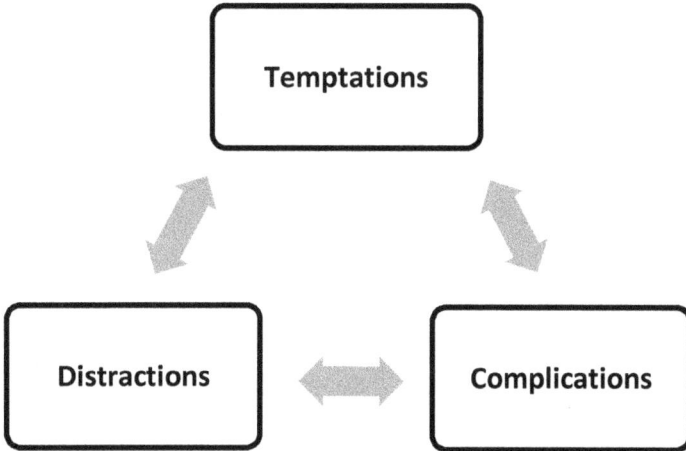

```
                    ┌─────────────────┐
                    │   Temptations   │
                    └─────────────────┘
                      ↗             ↘
    ┌─────────────────┐            ┌─────────────────┐
    │   Distractions  │  ⟷         │  Complications  │
    └─────────────────┘            └─────────────────┘
```

The third cycle is the result:

pride, anger, desire, want, sadness, jealousy, drugs, envy, hate, selfishness, kill, need, unfaithfulness, rage, self-pity, addiction, alcoholism, boredom, obsession, confusion, destruction, lying, failing marriage, self-indulgence, intolerance, vengeance, manipulation, cheating, suspicion, negativity, frivolity, greed...disconnection from God.

It's that simple...and it all starts with Ignorance, Laziness, Indifference, and Forgetfulness.

You expected The Enemy's plans to be pretty complicated against you, right?

Not really...

His genius lies in the simplicity of his tactics: he uses the weight of YOUR OWN Ignorance, Laziness, Indifference, and Forgetfulness to infect your mindset, as if "...a millstone were hung around his neck and he were cast into the sea (Luke 17:2 ESV)..."

Along with Temptation-Distraction-Complication, you limit your understanding of your incredible gift of communication; from that point, any spiritual communication related to God can be cut, and your miracle of a natural and spiritually-joyful life in Christ's salvation is lost in a living cycle of disconnection.

Spreading Like A Virus

Ignorance, Laziness, Indifference, and Forgetfulness are viral; they can spread from one person to another, even from one generation to the next:

"Do not be deceived: bad company corrupts good morals (1 Corinthians 15:33 NAS)..." and:

"He who walks with wise men will be wise, but the companion of fools will suffer harm (Proverbs 13:20 NAS)..."

A Master Of Execution

Once you have become a casualty of his Weapons Of Total Chaos,

The Enemy cleverly sets the right complex circumstances to keep your attention away from God.

And that's all he needs to do!

He sets the traps, but it is YOU WHO WALKS INTO THEM because Ignorance-Laziness-Indifference-Forgetfulness have altered your mindset, disarming your ability to align yourself with God's Word and a supernatural lifestyle in Christ:

"...for if someone does not know how to manage his own household, how will he care for God's church (Timothy 3:5 ESV)?"

"They are darkened in their understanding, alienated for the life of God because of the ignorance that is in them, due to their hardness of heart (Ephesians 4:18 ESV)..."

At every turn, The Enemy will set up his cycle of destruction:

With Ignorance: you are left not knowing enough about God, His powerful Word, and the importance of your gift of communication;

With Laziness: you lack the drive to discover (or restore) what you did not know (or forgotten), namely, that God waits for your contact;

With Indifference: you grow disinterested in regaining the contact that was lost because you no longer care in doing the one thing God expects you to do: communicate with Him.

With Forgetfulness: you no longer remember the power behind your gift of communication in the physical and spiritual level, or even how to get it restored. Even if you do begin a desire to discover or restore your relationship with God, Satan will use his cycle of destruction to:

a) Prevent your understanding of your gift of communication;
b) Tempt you in making the wrong life-decisions and separate you from God;
c) Distract your communications with God, neutralizing the power of His Word in your life;
d) Complicate your life with all kinds of situations and further disrupting your communications effectiveness with God.

Early Understanding Of The Enemy's Formula

Satan's formula against you isn't any different from any other plan; just as you make plans, he does the same! If you knew ahead of time how The Enemy has planned his campaign against you, then you would understand:

a) his secret agenda (to cut-off your communications with God);
b) setting you up for disconnection (sabotaging your mindset with Ignorance-Laziness-Indifference-Forgetfulness);
c) keeping you disconnected through Temptation, Distraction, Complication...

And what's the result? You become another spiritual casualty...

As you read on, you are becoming more aware of the devil's formula to cut off your contact with The Creator, and the realization that he uses common, familiar, everyday life to achieve it; but his success against you comes from your lack of **KNOWING AND UNDERSTANDING THE ORDER** that he executes these elements!

By understanding The Enemy's cycle of destruction, you will come to understand how he manages to be successful in what he does against you...and against humanity.

Chapter 8

Too Much To Defend Against

Even if you try reconnecting with God, Satan's Weapons Of Total Chaos (Ignorance, Laziness, Indifference, and Forgetfulness) are already executing ambush-after-ambush against your mind and your thinking, with more Temptations, Distractions, and Complications added into your life to deepen your separation from Him:

"O Lord, how many are my foes! Many are rising up against me (Psalm 3:1-2, ESV)..."

It's easy for The Enemy to de-rail you: his conspiracy was pre-planned using Ignorance-Laziness-Indifference-Forgetfulness...

He likes to mix things up in your life by using circumstances to Tempt-Distract and Complicate you from regaining your communication with God; to Satan, separation from God, and His Savior on earth Jesus, is everything!

If he succeeds, then you become "another notch on his belt," and this is what The Enemy wants all along: keep you from God, Jesus Christ, the Word, the promised salvation, your heartfelt joy, and the supernatural blessings intended for you!

God Knows What You Need...but so does The Enemy!

Every human being wants to feel safe and secure, lacking in nothing. It feels as if you are connected to something:

a) have enough money in the bank account;
b) make sure that your fridge is well supplied with food;
c) job security;
d) your kids are healthy and well cared for;
e) enjoy the 'good life', etc...

Satan knows this too, and wants you to feel connected, **BUT NOT TO GOD**, connecting you to other ideas and events that will set the stage of your spiritual distraction through:

pride, anger, desire, want, sadness, jealousy, drugs, envy, hate, selfishness, kill, needs, unfaithfulness, rage, self-pity, addiction, busy schedules, self-image, competition, obligations, bills, ego, job, alcoholism, boredom, obsession, confusion, destruction, lying, failing-marriage, self-indulgence, intolerance, vengeance, manipulation, cheating, suspicion, negativity, frivolity, greed, money, power, ambition, security...

The Deceiver has the ability to divert your trust away from God; he will infiltrate your fears and insecurities by setting up your mind to a lifestyle of constant uncertainty.

These days, "constant uncertainty" means:

i)   not enough money (even though you may have enough);
ii) not enough popularity (your ego wants more);
iii) not enough inner peace;
iv) not enough job security;
v)   not enough superiority;
vi) not enough status...etc.

Add to this (examples):

a) how to be better-off than your neighbor;
b) concerned about being the boss' favorite worker;
c) better-off than other family members;
d) show yourself better-off than strangers;
e) better dressed than the others;
f) having a nicer car;
g) possess a better home;
h) a larger pool;
i) a nicer watch...etc.

It is only natural to want all the good things that life has to offer, and you do deserve them...

Even God wants you to enjoy your life:

"For I know the plans I have for you, declares the Lord, plans for welfare and not for evil, to give you a future and a hope (Jeremiah 29:11)..."

BUT:

If your wants and desires take priority over your relationship with

God, then The Enemy has successfully diverted your attention from God's good intentions for you; all your blessings for a balanced life full of supernatural abundance, prosperity, restoration, and salvation-joy vanish...

And even if you do find success without God, you will find that your success is somehow missing something...

You've seen it happen all around you: successful people who have offered themselves certain liberties: fallen to the burden of drugs, infidelities, domestic violence, boredom, meaninglessness of life, etc...it affects them either personally, their loved ones, or both.

Yes, even a 'normal life' can be a deception; you are limited to living a natural life without feeling the infinite rush of joyful victory that comes from your spiritual side...

Understand how The Enemy works (it merits to briefly repeat what was covered in Chapter 7):

1) The Enemy will LIMIT YOUR UNDERSTANDING behind your purpose-built ability to communicate (Ignorance); he will keep you in the dark about this life-changing power in you, paralysing the effects of God's Word in your life and Jesus as your personal savior. You are left defenseless;

2) Without realizing the powerful potential of your gift of communication, your worries and responsibilities in your life will pile up without any supernatural assistance. Meanwhile, you press onward to tackle the challenges of life; on a spiritual level you sense that being mindful of God is a chore you don't feel like

thinking about, pushing it aside to "deal with it later on (you fall into Laziness);"

3) Maybe your expectations in life have not yet come; you get disappointed, even blaming God for your circumstances. You don't care about the Him because He 'hasn't delivered the goods' you expected; or you may have reached prosperity without God so you don't care about Him (Indifference);

4) With all the worries, burdens, even material successes, you drift away from God as you are involved in your challenges of life; instead, you turn solely to doing things so that you can either be admired, or simply to glorify yourself and your personal ambitions: your memory of Him and His involvement in your life are no longer remembered (Forgetfulness).

The result: there is no longer any meaningful contact with God; you've replaced God with career, objects of value, personal status, and other idols...

Chapter 9

God is Not....

So who is God to you?

As a spiritual person, you know who God is, but do you know **who He is not**?

If you do not, then you are open to Satan's Weapons Of Total Chaos regardless of how well you know the Bible!

By now, you are clearly aware that The Deceiver's prime target is to distort your God-given ability to communicate effectively, *especially* in the spiritual world; it is your destiny to have a fabulous spiritually personal relationship with the Lord...and Satan doesn't want that to happen!

Satan's plan is simple: create in you the wrong perception of God by using Ignorance, Laziness, Indifference, and Forgetfulness to create misconceptions in you; it's time for you to understand what are the common misconceptions...

What God Is Not

1) He Is Not Part-Time (as The Enemy wants you to think)

God is not a 'part-time God', so why does the world treat Him like one...?

He is not an occasional god that is 'kept in the closet' on 'stand-by' for when the need arises.

If you are treating Him like your convenience-tool only when you need Him or when your schedule demands, then God isn't listening to you...

Not that He doesn't want to...He does, and His "line is open..."

Problem is He can't hear you...you are not 'tuned-in' to Him if you treat Him as a 'part-time' God...would your husband/wife, or friends listen to you if you treat them like 'part-time' persons?

2) Like a Genie-In-A-Bottle

As a loving father, the Lord is there to assist you through difficult situations and bless your success ("...not a hair on your head will perish..." Luke 21:18)...

Unfortunately, billions from all faiths treat Him like some genie-in-a-bottle who waits for your command; some folks even pray selfish prayers: for fame, glory, money, the death of another, hateful vengeance, excuse for terrorism...

When their requests are not answered, they get angry, feel rejected, or worse: they get spiritually depressed, discouraged, and abandon God because He didn't deliver on their prayers exactly as they wanted...

Is it possible that you have made God into a genie, someone you think will "jump on your command?"

If so, then you are disconnected from God.

3) God Is Not 'Customer Service'

Many treat the Lord as some help-desk clerk; in their desperation, they vent their frustrations on Him.

It has to do with one's attitude; some folks out there see Him as a "back-door deal-maker" that will satisfy their particular whims. They do not proceed to ask Him as a loving father, but more like "customer service..."

It doesn't work:
God "doesn't do credit..."
God "doesn't take refunds or exchanges..."

God gives freely to those who place Him first within their heart, mind, and soul; so when you demand favors from God as if He is there to service you, then you set yourself up for disconnection.

4) God Is Not 'The Complaint Department'

Sometimes you can't help feeling like you want to let your emotions out on God for your difficult situations...even get angry at Him for "letting you down."

The Enemy wants you to get angry with God, and to unleash your frustrations against Him (example: "God, why don't you make me rich?" or "the neighbour has more than I," or "why can't I get a lucky break" etc...?).

Ignorance-Laziness-Indifference-Forgetfulness play a significant role here to set the stage for corrupting your communications; they de-tune your mind to focus on things such as worry, lack, hate, envy, cheating, selfishness, anger...and then you turn against God for not satisfying your personal desires. Complaining to God is ineffective communication because your mindset becomes confrontational against Him; you are already assuming that God has no connection with you: you've already made a conclusion that no inner peace or blessings are coming your way, only trouble.

You have limited the power of your communication, resulting in: dissatisfaction, hurt pride, unsatisfied selfish ambition, anger, etc...the results of Ignorance-Laziness-Indifference and Forgetfulness (as was discussed in the Introduction).

It is especially true when Forgetfulness make you lose sight that:

"...your Father knows what you need before you ask Him (Matthew 6:8, NIV)..."

5) God Isn't Waiting For You To Make Contact

The Enemy wants you to face the world alone with your problems and challenges...the loneliest person on earth. Every person on the planet feels that way at times, thanks to Satan's Weapons Of Total Chaos.

Ignorance-Laziness-Indifference-Forgetfulness can isolate you from God, and even Tempt you in believing that the Lord doesn't have time for you. It can lead to a negative mindset, distracting you away from the power you already had since the day you were born (your ability to communicate), becoming indifferent and forgetful that:

"...the Lord waits to be gracious to you (Isaiah 30:18, ESV)..."

6) God has His back turned to you...nothing to do with you

The Deceiver wants you trapped in constant cycles of Temptation-Distraction-Complication; he is constantly feeding you the idea that God is not interested in you as you struggle through life...

The Enemy wants you to forget that *God would actually intervene in your life* and its various circumstances; The Enemy wants you to ignore any hope that the Lord may be even slightly interested in your communication, and it makes you want to question God's dedication to you:

"...my God, why have you forsaken me? Why are you so far from saving me, so far from my cries of anguish? My God, I cry out by day, but you do not answer, by night, but I find no rest (Psalm 22:1-2)..."

Without hoping for any blessings and favor in your life, you may be Tempted to think that you are not worthy of God's attention; you may think you've been so bad that even God can't possibly want to hear from a person like you...

Such a satanic distraction from God's actual interest in you can lead you into a spiritual void:

1) Victim of Ignorance by misunderstanding God's willingness to
   help;

2) Energy-drained (Lazy) to contact God;
3) Indifferent because you wrongfully think He is indifferent to you;
4) Forgetful of God...

The very Temptation of thinking that God is not interested in you will definitely invite other Complications in your life...which can only reinforce in your mind that God does not want you to contact Him.

This is what Satan wants: make you believe that you are an outsider; God wants nothing to do with you, no contact, and any communication is hopeless.

And to perfect his spiritual crime, The Enemy must keep you away from the most fearful threat to his evil plot: Jesus.

Chapter 10

Jesus

Who is Jesus to you?

a) your savior?
b) your mentor?
c) your teacher?
d) your hero?
e) your coach?
f) your re-connector to personal communications to God?

He could be all the above, but most important, Jesus is your source of personal re-connection to God; He is the only one in the entire history of humankind that removes the clutter of spirituality and makes faith simple and easy. Of course The Enemy wants to distort all knowledge you may have of Christ; by doing so, he will cut off the only Source (Jesus) that could re-align your communications back to God in the simplest and easiest way...

Satan wants you to forget that Christ:

1)Was sent by God to save the world (John 3:17, NIV);
2) Restore: ("all...will be added to you...(Matthew 6:33, ESV);"
3) Shows you what to do ("Follow me...(Matthew 4:19, ESV);"

4) Shows you how to be "fishers of men...(Matthew 4:19, ESV);"
5) Was so connected with God's Spirit, that Jesus healed the sick...
6) Raised the dead...
7) Remained connected, even when Satan tried to corrupt him...
8) Never sought glory for himself (Matt. 4:8-10 NIV);
9) Supported peace: "Be at peace (Mark 9:50, NAS);"
10) Never abusive;
11) Compassionate, forgiving (eg: Luke 23:34, Mark 11:25...);
12) Sacrificed: "...lay down his life..." (John 15:1, NIV...);
13) Showed you how to talk with God (Luke 11:1);
14) Said to ask, knock, and receive blessings...(Matthew 7:7)...

In other words, The Enemy wants to keep you in a "spiritual communications black-out" as it was before, and sadly, after Christ:

(i) No realization that Christ is the Re-connector (Ignorance);
(ii) No efforts to know Jesus' as your re-connector (Laziness);
(iii) Disinterested in his message of freedom (Indifference);
(iv) Not mindful of Jesus at all in your life (Forgetfulness).

Add to this Temptations-Distractions and Complications that are designed to distance you from Jesus even further; it can leave you wide open to a complex maze of misinterpretations, generalizations, and different spiritual views that give you a distorted sense of spirituality...

You end up not only being cut-off from Jesus' easy intentions for you...

More importantly, you are cut-off from his keys of spiritual communications that God designed for YOU!

56

Jesus, The Gift The Enemy Does Not Want you To Have

Jesus arrived with a simple, uncomplicated blueprint to a peaceful and progressive lifestyle, blessed and supported supernaturally by God himself...and Satan does not want you to have it!

Even today (and amazingly), the world still cannot understand Jesus: Satan's Weapons Of Total Chaos (ie Ignorance, Laziness, Indifference, and Forgetfulness) are distracting folks away from knowing Jesus as your connection to boosting (or re-activating) your communications with God!

There is a test to find out if you've been separated from Jesus:

a) Do you feel a joy for being in a personal relationship with God?
b) A relief that you are at peace because you trust God?
c) Giddy as if you've won a million dollar lottery?
d) Looking to God with childlike love and security (eg:Luke18:17)?
e) Understood Jesus' message love and gratitude?
f) Circumstances mysteriously inexplicably resolved?
g) You feel a "spiritual stamina" and not deeply troubled by your current problems (or any unforeseen situations)?
h) A sense of inner freedom you never felt before?

If not, then The Enemy is interfering in your relationship with God...

Jesus...The Communication Link That Satan Wants Cut

Through His short ministry, Jesus revealed a crystal-clear line of communication to God for you...a supernatural access that:

i) uncomplicates the complicated;
ii) helps you re-establish uninterrupted contact with God;
iii) a Father-to-child style of relationship...

No wonder He invites everyone to:

"Follow me...(Luke 9:59)," and:

"...Take my yoke upon you and learn from me, for I am gentle and humble in heart, and you will find rest for your soul. For my yoke is easy and my burden light (Matthew 11:28-30, NIV)."

"Gentle and humble in heart..." You see, Jesus' guidance is not just another complicated and enforced spiritual idea you must submit to; He restores in you a simple and clear line of communication to God at the sharpest focus that best combines with your human nature...

It resembles a family-style relationship: Father to son/daughter...

The Enemy wants you to think the opposite: that your contact with God is that of a master-to-slave mentality, that God is a ruthless yet compassionate master over His creation. Under the heavy burden of Ignorance-Laziness-Indifference-Forgetfulness, The Deceiver will expose you to a complicated wasteland of ideologies that are meant to bog down any personal relationship with God...

Is this happening to you right now? Are you looking for a level of spirituality, but it "religion" makes it too complex for you?

Make no mistake: you will be driven to inquire other ideologies and spiritual rituals that mimic faith in God...only that there is no interactive contact with the spiritual. Your faith becomes just long-winded volumes of words, and sometimes enforced rituals that amount only to "mental and intellectual entertainment."

Some call it "playing religion," and no real contact with God...

From looking at the present circumstances around the world, Satan's deceit has not been detected or fully understood. The world continues to fall victim to Satan's Weapons Of Total Chaos:

1) Jesus is not seen as the gentle Savior;
2) God's Word in Christ is ignored for other "feel good" ideas;
3) Prayers are not getting answered;
4) Feeling cut-off from the spiritual, trapped in the natural;
5) Turmoil and suffering continues, ignoring Christ's message;
6) Wars waged...fear and terror reigns.

Miracles: God's Powerful Message in Jesus

Jesus demonstrated the power of communication during His ministry through miracles. They were not intended to be some magician's sideshow as The Enemy wants you to believe...

It was all about communication at a higher level:

The healing of the sick, the raising of the dead, making the paralyzed walk, etc...all this was a direct demonstration of Christ's unique communication-relationship in the spiritual realm...a relationship He wants to share with you!

Jesus himself mentioned His intentions for your sake:

"...believe in God, believe also in me...I go to prepare a place for you...(John 14:2 NKJ)"

And if you had any doubts about Jesus in relation to God, He said:

"...believe Me for the sake of the works themselves... (John 14:11, NKJ)"

You see from above that even Jesus offers you the free choice to judge his intentions, by observing the works that he did (the good works of healing, hope, love...).

Jesus The Savior...and Satan's Sworn Enemy

When Jesus walked the earth, some people at that time thought that He was a savior sent to liberate the region from the grip of the Roman Empire who occupied the area during that time; establish a new political order so to speak.

They expected the "Savior" to be a revolutionary, a violent person; they expected protest and war as a means to freedom..

They were wrong even before Jesus' ministry had begun, their minds pre-programmed in "Stone Age" thinking, that there was no other salvation than violence and revolution...

Yet Christ had a more valuable mission, the same as it is today: to bring you to an understanding of what is expected of you and get your own spiritual communications back on-line with God freely and easily...

That's what a REAL Savior does!

The Enemy however wants dis-harmony in you; he wants you conflicted, resulting in the disruption of communications with God...to cause separation, forceful religious submission, a dark mindset...an opposite effect from Christ Jesus.

Just look at the state of the world today...

The Enemy uses Ignorance-Laziness-Indifference-Forgetfulness to extinguish Jesus from your life.

Look how clever this is: The Deceiver will manipulate your God-given free will to steer you in a life that has no easy spiritual direction, clogged-up in your daily grind of life...

Destroying Your Trust In God's Champion

Satan's Weapons of Total Chaos is all about separation: cutting off of your spiritual/natural gift to communicate, reducing it into a low level ability. Your communications become only something that you use on earth...no spiritual effect.

As you become infected with the daily grind, your heart hardens with your tough experiences in life. Easy instructions from Jesus such as:

"Ask and you shall receive...Seek, and you shall find...Knock, and the door shall be opened (Luke11:9, NIV)..." and:

"Love one another. As I have loved you, so you must love one another (John 13:34, NIV)..."

...are ignored.

The Enemy knows that Jesus is the key to re-igniting your incredible ability to communicate with God. Satan wants your mindset, your attitude, your thinking to be infected by the cares and worries of the world; that the spiritual cannot help you in the daily concerns of your life...that you can't trust in the spiritual...

He makes you distrust God's Fatherly devotion to you, and:

1) prevents you from trusting that Jesus can help;
2) doubting that your salvation-joy is implanted within you;
3) mis-aligning your communications with God;
4) skeptical about receiving blessings and favor;
5) making you believe that salvation isn't meant for you...

The Enemy employs psychological warfare to discredit Jesus in any way possible, making you lose trust; he doesn't want you to recognize Jesus' supernatural ability to bridge your gap to God. He does this by Tempting you into Distractions that trivialize, even ignore Jesus and His Goodwill mission.

You see, The Enemy knows the incredible spiritual power dormant inside you and knows that Jesus can re-activate this ability...

He also knows how easy it is to Distract you from understanding your great potential...by simply re-aligning your thinking away from Jesus, and into other things (useless rituals, forceful religions, and 'feel-good' ideologies)...and effectively neutralizing your spiritual communications.

Yes, your naturally-born ability to communicate is powerful, but at the same time extremely vulnerable to Temptation, Distraction, and Complication. This is what Satan counts on, by:

1) Mis-aligning you with Ignorance-Laziness-Indifference
   Forgetfulness;
2) Adding Temptations-Distractions-Complications in your life;
3) Keeping you from understanding Jesus' message on how to
   reconnect with God;
4) Separating you from God's supernatural intervention in your life;
5) Promises of favor, blessings, divine prosperity...unrealistic.

The Enemy knows that without Jesus to reactivate your spiritual
communications, what follows is a life encased in a hard shell of
bitterness, enforcement, submission, degredation, intolerance, hate,
violence, self-serving agendas, superficial religious rites,
etc...Satan's intended path for all.

Chapter 11

Christ Within You...Satan's Main Target Overall

As a follower of Christ, you are a part of a supernatural movement of spiritual revival and restoration of the highest freedom that is rarely felt in the natural world.

By having freely invited Jesus as your personal savior and instructor, you are in fact opening the door to an incredible opportunity; to ignite within you an ability has been implanted in you from the moment you began to exist, but remains suppressed:

Your incredible power of communication!

Your ability to communicate has awesome potential in both the natural and spiritual world...once properly released!

Even Jesus talks about your incredible potential:

"Is it not written in your Law, 'I have said you are gods'" (John 10:34-35, NIV) ?

Jesus was referring to Psalm 82:6, that:

"I said, 'You are gods; you are all sons of the Most High."

But The Enemy does not want that privilege for you. He wants you:

1) Spiritually suppressed;
2) To view your relationship to God as Master and slave;
3) Unsaved, a pawn for God's indulgent pleasure;
4) A slave to doubt and uncertain of God in your life;
5) Undeserving of blessings and favor in your life;
6) No inner empowerment embedded in you;
7) Ignorant, Lazy, Indifferent, and Forgetful of Jesus...

This is ALL CONTRARY TO YOUR NATURE which desires:

a) Spiritual freedom;
b) To view your relationship with God as Father-to-child;
c) Saved by Christ, protected by God;
d) Assurance of God's presence in your life;
e) Expectation of blessings and favor to be released;
f) Empowered;
g) To be knowledgeable, active, interested, and mindful;

The Deceiver doesn't want you awakened to your incredible inner power to communicate beyond the natural and into the supernatural; instead, he wants you to believe that your life is ordinary and suppressed in the daily grind of life where:

1) Your life is a constant hopeless struggle;
2) You are too far gone for any spiritual reconnection;
3) Undeserving of spiritual salvation or compassion;
4) That you are unforgivable;
5) No redemption...

6) That Christ's message of spiritual freedom isn't for you;
7) Blessings and favor are for others, not you...
8) That you are not worth it;
9) Following Jesus is wrong;
10) Not chosen to live the message;
11) You are not part of God's Winners' Circle.

Equipped with Ignorance-Laziness-Indifference-Forgetfulness, followed by Temptation-Distraction-Complication, The Enemy deceives you in thinking that Christ has nothing to do with bringing out the implanted, inner potential in you...

Satan wants you to "play religion" when in fact you are hopelessly lost in the natural world; to pursue your spirituality with irrelevant, "feel-good" religious rituals. No real restoration of communication with God or any realization of your true importance as part of a great supernatural communications network...

Just as someone tries to discourage you to pursue your ambitions (example: "forget about opening your business...you don't have what it takes; you're not good enough for medical school; you are not qualified...etc), The Enemy does not want you to pursue a "cutting-edge" faith where your inner power of communication is revived and turns your life into a wonderful miracle!

Rules And Complications

With all the great advancements in the world, life has become convenient and fun; but it can also become a complicated mess...and you can see how complex life has become with all the rules/regulations, volumes of 'fine-print' and so many things to do with so little time...

It is also the perfect breeding-ground for Satan's Weapons Of Total Chaos (ie Ignorance, Laziness, Indifference, and Forgetfulness)! By drowning you in a sea of Temptations-Distractions and Complications, Satan can distance you from reviving your incredible potential within you by:

1) Not knowing Jesus' message of revival (Ignorance);
2) Not wanting to spend energy reviving your faith (Laziness);
3) Not interested in reviving your incredible ability (Indifference);
4) Not remembering the awesome potential in you (Forgetfulness)...

It's easy to get you off-course with the rush of today's modern life and all the good and bad that comes along with it. This is why the simple message of Christ's freedom and inner revival can be an attractive alternative in today's world...but The Enemy doesn't like that: he wants you to be suppressed and enslaved!

Ever wonder why Jesus said:

"...take my yoke upon you and learn from me, for I am gentle and humble in heart, and you will find rest for your souls. For my yoke is easy and my burden is light (Matthew 11:29-30, NIV)..?"

Jesus wants you to toss your negative mindset of burden away, and release in you an enlightened and revived spirit...

Meanwhile, The Destroyer wants your inner self overwhelmed in complications so that you become far removed from God's Winners' Circle. He will apply the full force of Ignorance-Laziness-Indifference-Forgetfulness in your life, reinforced with Temptation,

Distraction, and Complication to keep you away from the regenerative words that Jesus spoke.

The Enemy wants you to follow his own rules:

a) Ignore God.
b) Forget Jesus.
c) Don't follow Jesus' teachings.
d) Jesus' message of freedom is not important.
e) No spiritual freedom in the natural world.
f) God does not listen to you.
g) You will never reconnect to God.
h) You are wasting time reading the Word in the Bible.
i) Supernatural intervention doesn't exist.
j) Follow a different message other than Christ.
k) There is no inner potential waiting to be released in you...

He wants you to be forever in doubt of Christ's Good News Message; he wants you trapped, suppressed, enslaved, seeking dead-end answers elsewhere that will lead you away from becoming part of God's Winners' Circle...

Chapter 12

Your Faith Is Under Attack

Your faith in God is measured on:

1. how mindful you are of Him, and:
2. how you communicate your mindfulness to Him.

It's that simple! Your unconditional desire to communicate with God determines the blessings that pour into your life (more on this later in Part Two, The Solution: Restoring Communications).

The Enemy however has other plans for your faith: to be in constant attack with the purpose of cutting you off from God through Ignorance-Laziness-Indifference-Forgetfulness. Along with Temptation-Distraction and Complication in your daily life, Satan diverts your mind into believing that all spiritual pursuits make no logical sense:

"The person without the Spirit does not accept the things that come from the Spirit of God but considers them foolishness, and cannot understand them because they are discerned only through the Spirit (1 Corinthians 2:14, NIV)."

Sabotaging your Trust In God

Ever heard of the experiment years ago where you let yourself fall backward into the arms of another person? It was an experiment on how far you would trust someone. You really need to trust someone to allow yourself to fall backwards that way...

Your trust in God should be the same, trusting that He is there to catch you from falling:

"Do not fear, only believe. (Mark 5:36, ESV)"

Yet for countless folks out there, trusting God is getting harder and harder; they have no confidence that He is there to catch them if they fall victim to some kind of circumstance. Sometimes they feel they have been touched by blessings, and some other times they wonder where God's mercy has gone...

In other words, they are communicating doubt:

"...one who doubts is like a wave of the sea that is driven and tossed by the wind. For that person must not suppose that he receive anything from the Lord; he is a double-minded man, unstable in all his ways (James 1:6-8, ESV)."

Doubting God's ability to intervene in your daily life is an indicator that Satan's Weapons Of Total Chaos have attacked your mindset and has weakened both your understanding and doubting your trusting relationship with the Lord in your natural and spiritual life.

Natural And Spiritual Life

When you decide to live your life without any contact with God, you are placing your faith into the natural life...in other words you place your destiny in yourself, and to chance. No divine intervention in the picture. You are in control of everything, and nothing else exists other than yourself, your own personal efforts, and random variables (in other words, luck) that can work for or against you; in a way, your spiritual life is essentially dead:

"...you were dead in your transgressions and sins, in which you used to live when you followed the ways of this world and the ruler of the kingdom of the air, the spirit who is now at work in those who are disobedient. All of us also lived among them at one time, gratifying the cravings of our flesh and following its desires and thoughts (Ephesians 2:1-4, NIV)..."

Satan wants you to think that the supernatural is far removed from your reality, especially if you add all your earthly pleasures, challenges and pressures...further reinforcing your doubt that God is is not interested in you.

Communication is Key...The Enemy Wants You Cut Off

You've heard that staying in communication with those you love is critical to healthy and long-lasting relationships; communicating spiritually with God is exactly the same thing. Satan wants you to ignore this important parallel and to forget about your extraordinary level of communication that is waiting to emerge from within you.

How will he achieve this? He will get you to question the

usefullness of your faith by applying Ignorance-Laziness-Indifference-Forgetfulness at **an early stage in your life**...

Oftentimes, his attacks against you start BEFORE you were born...by disconnecting your parents with their own Ignorance-Laziness-Indifference-Forgetfulness. It may even go as far back as your grandparents and their parents, etc...so that the joy of blessings and prosperity that God promised would be lost, for generations!

Imagine, generations of human souls lost because they ignored the spiritual...attacked by Satan's Weapons of Total Chaos, and Tempting them into Distractions that brought distortion in their spiritual communications!

Destroying the World...by Destroying the Word

Satan never defeated Jesus...Jesus is God's Communications Champion, and you would want to learn faith in God from His Undisputed Champion!

The Enemy understood the importance of Christ, and wanted to destroy His Good News message...by destroying God's Messenger (Christ).

Satan failed of course; but he now re-directs his attacks to destroy YOU by preventing Jesus to enter into your life through clever use of Ignorance-Laziness-Indifference and Forgetfulness!

Add to this Temptations-Distractions and Complications...and your disconnection from God becomes complete!

The Enemy's attacks are relentless; he continues to discredit Jesus' simple message of freedom and salvation-joy to an unsuspecting world by implanting Ignorance-Laziness-Indifference and Forgetfulness; setting up your mind to think your communication with God is ineffective, that it just doesn't work. His ultimate goal: cut you off from key points of contact that bring alive your communications with God (to be covered in Part Two)...

Attacking Your Trust In Your Own Communication

Faith is believing that you have a communications-line open to God and trusting that He is listening. It's another way of saying that you are communicating your trust that God can intervene in your life...the very qualities that The Enemy wants to destroy in you.

If you have any doubt of your communications-relationship with God, then you are sending a weak signal to the spiritual; and as in all weak signals, chances are that God cannot hear you.

Using a barrage of circumstances to Tempt-Distract and Complicate your life away from God and Jesus, The Enemy will deceitfully make you believe that your prayer-communications do not bring any response from God...

There is a very thin line that separates 'meaningful' and 'meaningless' contact in God. All The Enemy needs to do is cut off your initial understanding about who you really are: that you are born to communicate at a physical AND spiritual level. If you do not have a sincere understanding that you are born to communicate in the spiritual world, then you will have no real connection with God...even though you still go through the earthly "motions and rituals of religion," but never ascending higher.

Empty Words

You can be misled to believe in your religion, but there is no weight to your faith other than demanding favors from God as if he is 'customer service...'

This is no communication to God; it is communication to yourself, your ego. This was discussed by Jesus, and instructs against it in the New Testament in Luke 18:

"...he who exalts himself will be humbled (Luke 18:14)..."

How is a person humbled? Prayers are not fully answered (if not at all), favor and blessings are not received, no supernatural intervention in your circumstances; any success is empty and meaningless.

With the glitter of the natural life enticing you to abandon your spiritual side, Ignorance-Laziness-Indifference-Forgetfulness (ie Satan's Weapons of Total Chaos) can turn genuine, heartfelt, uncompromising prayer-communication into heartless demands for selfish reasons, which is something that Satan tries to implant in you by Tempting, Distracting and Complicating circumstances.

The Enemy Wants You To Believe You Have No Power

Do you know that as a follower of Christ, you are privileged because:

Jesus UNCOMPLICATES and SIMPLIFIES your mindset and your

thinking, so you can send messages of joy to God, communicating total enjoyment of sharing your natural life with Him in the spiritual world.

Satan will naturally take the opposite position: he will distort your mind (due to Ignorance-Laziness-Indifference-Forgetfulness) in order to COMPLICATE and CONFUSE you, to make you underestimate and doubt your power of communication.

The Enemy wants your well-intentioned contact with God to be replaced with unfavored, unconfident, powerless, weak signals that will render your communication efforts for a personal relationship with the Lord ineffective.

It can reinforce in you the wrong idea that God is not listening to your prayer-communication. By Tempting you to believe that God is not listening, you become Distracted by your own hurt feelings; it can grow to a disatisfaction that can divert you into inescapable maze of negative thoughts and circumstances...and further distancing you from a close and personal relationship with God.

And it all started with a misunderstanding (or not knowing) of how important your gift of communications actually is! The Destroyer wants to you to be unaware, even forget that **you are an essential member in God's communication network**:

a) you are not important to God (Ignorance);
b) supernatural communication is energy-draining (Laziness);
c) not to pay attention to spiritual contact with God (Indifference);
d) God and His Word has no place in your daily life
   (Forgetfulness).

Here Is A Twist: You Are Important...to Satan

The Enemy loves to have you around, especially when he can manipulate your destiny through Ignorance-Laziness-Indifference-Forgetfulness; he will then bury you in a sea of Temptations-Distractions and Complications, and finally: keep you away from Jesus!

He will even support other distorted religious convictions that turn everything spiritual into turmoil, such as:

Kill in the name of God;
Die in the name of God;
Hate in the name of God;
Enslave in the name of God;
Your soul is not saved in Christ;
Your spirit is not free;
That you have not won the battle of the Spirit...

Keep this in mind: The Deceiver wants to limit your understanding of your ability to communicate; he wants you to believe that communication is only a natural function, a biological thing, good to discover your world and that's it.

(Now pay attention) Satan will even *encourage you to live a good life in the natural*, but without God or Jesus in your life...

Remember that Satan FAILED to prevent Jesus from sharing the powerful message of reconciliation with God, a message that shook the foundations of the world (even to this day). But The Enemy can still bring failure to Jesus' message from being understood and shared...

Chapter 13

Prayer-Communication Disrupted

In Christian life, prayer is an act of heartfelt communication with God, an opportunity to 'tune-in' with Him; it is a moment for spiritually intimate interaction with the Lord.

The Enemy wants none of that; just as a 'third person' who wants to interfere in your relationships, Satan wants to 'get in the way' and sabotage your relationship with God. He knows how powerful your prayer communication can become when you are 'spiritually tuned-in...' all kinds of wonderful events begin to manifest!

Satan's agenda is to ensure that you will never get to that personal level of communicating with the Lord...!

Communication Gone Astray

Nowadays, prayer-communications to God look more like:

1) demands on your own terms;
2) 'making deals with God;'
3) ordering God to do something for you;
4) part of your 'to-do' list;
5) God slotted into your "tight time-schedule;"

6) as if 'ordering something from a store-catalog;'
7) impatient, selfish demands...

One of Satan's main objectives is to make you lose your prayer-communication effectiveness. He will use his core tools at his disposal that are in fact your source of weakness (and now you know about them): Ignorance, Laziness, Indifference, and Forgetfulness to keep you away from being an effective prayer-communicator.

And he has plenty of "ammo" to make your communications go astray: situations in your life, your thinking (mindset)...all the challenges and attractions exposed to you in this world.

Mis-alignment

One of the biggest complaints you hear about God is that:

a) He does not hear your prayers;
b) that prayer-requests go unanswered;
c) your expectations of miracles fall short.

There are reasons why prayer-requests are not answered, and this deals directly with Ignorance-Laziness-Indifference-Forgetfulness:

1) Unaware of the 'spiritual blockers' (Ignorance);
2) Not putting the effort to detect them (Laziness);
3) Not caring about finding out (Indifference);
4) Not remembering to take action (Forgetfulness).

To disrupt your "spiritual-alignment" The Deceiver simply

shifts your thinking, and steering you away from communication alignment with Jesus and His Good News message; by doing so, Satan will successsfully do to you what he could not do in Jesus...cut you off from God.

Prayer-Requests...not replied

Satan can cut you off from God even if you are a believing Christian: Ignorance-Laziness-Indifference-Forgetfulness, along with Temptation-Distraction and Complication are working behind the scenes to mis-align your mindset as you wrestle with the aggravations and challenges of life that make you feel:

a) lost...instead of having won in Jesus;
b) not saved...instead of feeling reborn;
c) worried...instead of being joyful;
d) impatient...instead of sensing inner calm;
e) frustrated...instead of living satisfied;
f) egotistical...instead of humble;
g) overwhelmed...instead of in-control;
h) negative-minded...instead of positive-minded;
i) lonely...instead of belonging...

He starts it all by blocking you from the truth about your incredible gift of communication. Sadly, this area has been seriously neglected, leaving many well-intentioned believers to struggle with their faith needlessly because they do not realize how critical their power of communications really is in both the natural and spiritual life...

It starts with Ignorance...ignorance of your prayer-communication disruption. As far as you are concerned, everything is normal, you believe in God, and nothing is distorted...but you feel disconnected and this makes you feel bewildered, a bit confused, doubtful...

It was already discussed previously: The Destroyer prepares your fall from God's promised blessings in your life by using his Weapons Of Total Chaos; it is a planned mis-alignment than can go back even before you were born, to your grandparents and beyond:

"For I do not want you to be ignorant of the fact, brothers, that our forefathers were all under the cloud (1 Corinthians 10:1, NIV)..."

You've Just Made A New God

Real prayer is an expression of inner yearning to reach out in spiritual contact; it is implanted within you, and God wants you to use it to get in contact with Him...an element that The Enemy wants to sabotage.

Everyone has a need to communicate at some level, and this includes the spiritual; anyone who doesn't communicate with God usually connects with someone or something else...it could be other dieties, ideologies, objects, movie-stars, etc. in order to satisfy the mysterious psychological need for connection...even if the connection leads to nowhere.

Once your communication with God is mis-aligned and takes second place in your life (sometimes last place...sometimes no place), your problems and daily issues become your priority. You connect solely to your daily issues and challenges that have absorbed your concentration, while God is pushed aside:

80

"For those who live according to the flesh set their minds on the things of the flesh (Romans 8:5, NIV)..."

It seems sensible to place your priorities of life first; after all, you have debts to pay, raising kids, obligations to your work, personal concerns, etc. Clearly there is nothing wrong with being a responsible person...it is expected of you. This is where The Enemy applies his spiritual mis-alignment: he cleverly and discretely disconnects you from God, and connects your whole self entirely to your circumstances...

In other words, you have just made yourself a new god: your problems, your ambitions, your paycheck, your riches, your revenge, your personal possessions, yourself, your drug addiction, etc...!

Well, guess what: you've been disconnected...and that's just fine with Satan!

Chapter 14

The Bible: Banned by Satan

Do you know why the Holy Bible is considered the greatest book ever to be published?

1) It's your 'how-to' manual of intimate contact to God;
2) It offers simple and quick solutions;
3) It's easy to read;
4) Based entirely on Love:

"All scripture is given by inspiration of God, and is profitable for doctrine, for reproof, for correction, for instruction in righteousness: That the man of God may be perfect, thoroughly furnished unto all good works (2 Timothy 3:16-17, KJV)."

The Enemy does not want you to know about the Bible as your how-to guide. He knows the Bible is the KEY that opens up your supernatural contact with God to a deep and personal level...

The Bible:

i)   trains...The Enemy wants you weak;

ii)   prepares...Satan wants you vulnerable;

iii) sensitizes...he wants you numb and indifferent;

iv)   provides...he wants you lacking;

v)   simplifies...Satan wants you complicated and lost;

vi)   gives wisdom...Satan wants you ignorant;

vii) disciplines...he wants you out of control;

viii) liberates...he wants you enslaved;

ix)   strengthens...Satan wants you weak and lazy;

x)   releases the Holy Spirit Power...Satan wants to suppress it;

xi)   connects to God, and Jesus...The Enemy wants you cut off...

The Deceiver wants you to be permanently blocked off from God's Word as shared by Christ. Using various Temptations-Distractions and Complications in your life, The Enemy keeps you away from the supernatural enablement of the Word (Ignorance) by making you Lazy in pursuing the Word, Indifferent about what the Word can do for you, and even makes you Forget about the Bible.

The Enemy Does Not Want You To Read The Bible

Satan cannot stop you from reading the contents of the Bible (especially the New Testament); but he can block your full understanding of it by working on your mind, infecting it with Ignorance-Laziness-Indifference-Forgetfulness...distracting your thinking before you can even begin your journey.

He can set up your mind to doubt its encouraging words: Satan wants you to believe that the Word in the Bible is powerless; that they cannot manifest miracles and salvation-joy...all in order to distance you from loving the principal character in the Bible's New Testament: Jesus.

Follow Him...Not

Satan could not defeat Jesus, which makes Christ your personal spiritual champion, liberator, spiritual coordinator...the undisputed Champion of God and the world...

In other words, Jesus is your ultimate spiritual mentor whose instruction in the Bible brings to life your salvation and supernatural transformation!

The Enemy does not want you to reach that level of spirituality; he already knows that Christ is your reconnector to God, and tries to sabotage any interest in your reading about Him in your quest for revival.

He will do it by:

1) Making you believe that there is no supernatural salvation in Christ's instruction;
2) Distracting you away from Jesus' teachings in the Bible;
3) Spending less time discovering the Good News message of Christ;
4) Making you indifferent about Jesus entirely;
5) Getting you to forget how God's Divine Word comes alive in Christ;
6) Unable or unwilling to understand The Word;
7) Follow other ideas...

Jesus had something to say about this:

"Why is my language not clear to you? Because you are unable to hear what I say...(John 8:43-44, NIV)..."

Paul mentions it too:

"But the natural man receiveth not the things of the Spirit of God: for they are foolishness unto him (1 Corinthians 2:14, KJV)..."

Satan wants you banned from a supernatural experience with God by not understanding the deeper meaning of what Jesus is saying; he will even try to keep you from reading about Christ, by making Him seem 'out-of-date', 'boring', 'not fashionable', 'impossible to follow...'

(Author's personal comment: "boy, we need Jesus today more than any other period of history...!)

The Enemy would rather see you smothered in your own false sense of spiritual enlightenment by following "feel-good" rituals, "routine prayer" schedules, and other faiths in order to feel religious...all to keep you from understanding Jesus and His simple message of reconciliation with God...

The Word in the Bible is a source of constant threat to Satan and his plans for global domination. No wonder Christ's simple message is often targeted and persecuted around the world ever since the days of his ministry...The Enemy wants the Word in the Bible and Jesus out of the picture!

Jesus Is A Problem...To The Enemy

The Enemy knows that the New Testament in the Bible is your key to complete contact with God because of Jesus. He hates the idea that Christ is your mentor, your instructor, your re-connector; instead, he preoccupies you with challenges and circumstances to further increase your Ignorance-Laziness-Indifference and Forgetfulness, driving you away from the Jesus.

Jesus is a problem to The Enemy because:

Satan failed to defeat Jesus!

He cannot defeat God, did not defeat Jesus, and is unable to compromise the Spirit of God...

But, he can defeat YOU!

The Enemy will defeat you by keeping you away from the Bible that contains the "spiritual trigger" to your spiritual enablement: the "trigger" is Jesus Christ.

Scriptures And Verses...keys that Satan does not want you to know

The scriptures and verses in the New Testament section of the Bible are instructions...keys that lead you to discover your personal relationship with God.

It is not religion...

It is not procedural...

It is not oppression...

It merits to repeat this one more time:

(please read with an open mind)

"All scripture is given by inspiration of God, and is profitable for doctrine, for reproof, for correction, for instruction in righteousness: That the man of God may be perfect, thoroughly furnished unto all good works (2 Timothy 3:16-17, KJV)."

It's all about bringing out perfect righteousness in you...

"Are you saying that I'm not perfect?" you might ask.

No one is perfect in the natural world...living only in the natural deprives your heart, your soul, and your spirit of the mysterious perfection that comes from the blissful interaction between the natural **and** spiritual.

The words in the New Testament are meant to give you this balance, and they are power-packed, and DO WORK to bring supernatural blessings...words that The Enemy does not want you to understand or even use in your daily life.

Just open the New Testament at any page, and it will show you instructions to your reconnection to God.

The Enemy fears the power behind God's Word in the Bible. But he also knows that without heartfelt faithful trust in God, the Word does nothing for you. So for those that do read the Word and await supernatural results, you should know that The Destroyer will set the stage to disrupt your thinking and place doubt in your mind; to make you believe that the Word does nothing in your life, and to progressively separate you from God by Tempting-Distracting and Complicating your mind with thoughts of burdens and life-challenges:

"...your thoughts will be led astray from a sincere and pure devotion to Christ (2 Corinthians 11:3, NIV)..." and:

"For although they knew God, they did not honor him as God or give thanks to him, but they became futile in their thinking, and their foolish hearts were darkened (Romans 1:21, ESV)..."

Everyone desires some kind of spiritual connection to the universe; it's a built-in desire in you, as if an invitation for spiritual contact has been implanted within. On the one hand, Jesus had come to show you a simple and uncomplicated solution to spiritual contact and supernatural interaction with God; on the other hand, Satan's tactics sabotage your pursuit by distracting you:

"In their case the god of this world has blinded the minds of the unbelievers, to keep them from seeing the light of the gospel of the glory of Christ, who is the image of God (2 Corinthians 4:4, ESV)..."

Bible Study

What is Bible Study, really?

Just as you read a "User Manual", bible study is really about how-to re-align your mind and your thinking to a simpler way of self-discovery...revealing who (and what) you are: both a natural AND spiritual being empowered to communicate naturally and spiritually in this vast universe...

But Satan wants you to think that Bible Study is "doing tiresome homework" that you don't feel like doing; he will even make reading the Bible seem irrelevant for this modern time...

You might be determined to stay on course with your spiritual goals, but Satan's Weapons Of Total Chaos can take you off-course. Using Ignorance-Laziness-Indifference-Forgetfulness to steer you away from reading the Word (and Jesus' coaching), The Enemy can easily apply circumstances to Tempt-Distract and Complicate your life, and distance you from understanding the actual power of the Word:

a) the less you know about the Word, the less your spiritual connection (Ignorance);
b) not putting in the appropriate effort to understand and tap into the power of the Word (Laziness);
c) not caring to see the enormous difference it can make in your life (Indifference);
d) not remembering the awesome potential of the Word in your life (Forgetfulness)...

The Enemy sets the stage to keep you disconnected from the incredible power that God has set aside for you. He will go as far as infecting everything around you to assure your separation in advance: your parents (even grandparents and great grandparents), your changing circumstances, your community, friends, the good and bad, etc. can be used to set your stage of separation...

As a master deceiver, Satan knows human nature and how to manipulate your mind; plenty of folks, even those who believe, are decoyed away from the Bible because:

a) it takes away their "quality time;"

b) demanding deeper reflection you don't have time for;

c) it is pointless;

d) you are not interested;

e) you claim you know it's contents already;

f) you claim to know 'about life;'

g) it won't help your circumstances anyway;

h) it's "religion;"

i) There's "good stuff on t.v." instead, etc...

Once he succeeds to cloud your awareness of the incredible spiritual potential of the Word and Jesus in your life, the Word becomes ineffective; it becomes just like any other book, just words...

And The Destroyer's objective is to ban you from doing what Jesus had already said you could do:

"I tell you the truth, anyone who has faith in me will do what I have been doing. He will do even greater things than these...(John 14:12 ESV)"

Yes, Satan wants to prevent you from doing the great things that Jesus said you would do, by keeping you away from the powerful Word in the Bible.

Chapter 15

Introducing The Enemy

At this very moment Satan is working to disconnect you from God.

You are not alone; he's been doing so to billions of folks out there for generations!

Realize this: Satan knows that **YOU** are valuable to God...more valuable than you think; The Enemy knows more about you than you know yourself...

Even Jesus mentioned your value:

"Don't be afraid; you are worth more than many sparrows (Luke 12:7, NIV)..."

The Deceiver knows that:

a) YOU are the Lord's precious creation;
b) That God made YOU an instrument of communication;
c) The Lord is interested and waits to hear from YOU;

d) YOU are the reason God sent Jesus: to help release your communicative spirit and reach out to Him;

e) God showed YOU a simple way to restore your relationship with Him;

f) Jesus even demonstrated His communication with God himself, becoming the example so that YOU do the same;

g) YOU were worthy enough for Jesus to suffer on the cross (as prophesied);

h) YOU are the one that Jesus saved through His death and resurrection;

i) Jesus defeated The Enemy...for YOU!

Satan knows all this, and wants you to casually ignore it all; he is keenly interested in keeping you from finding your salvation through Jesus, because he knows that Christ is the key to your supernatural release...and his own defeat!

Satan's Simple Plan

Satan uses simple tactics to cause you disconnection from God. The simplicity is based on the premise that he knows human nature, and taps into the very heart of your Ignorance, Laziness, Indifference, and Forgetfulness to distance you from the supernatural power of the Word in Christ.

As a supernatural being himself, the Enemy knows what you know about yourself: he understands your ambitions for a good life, your personal goals...and he will use the good and the bad to get you out of touch with God.

He likes to feed humanity's misguided sense of pride and

invincibility by making you feel you don't need God or Jesus; he knows that plenty of folks out there presume to know everything that needs to be known about life, even spirituality. It is this egotistical and self-righteous presumption that The Enemy feeds on and brings spiritual disconnection that carries on from generation-to-generation, from one war to the next:

"For if a man think himself to be something, when he is nothing, he deceiveth himself (Galatians 6:3, KJV);"

"Pride goeth before destruction and a haughty spirit before a fall (Proverbs 27:2, KJV);

Satan doesn't really care if you love God, believe in God, or even trust in God...he only needs to make sure that **you are spiritually disconnected from God!**

Your life hangs on a very fine spiritual balance, and the devil knows how to destabilize it...especially these days with modern technology, modern conveniences, modern stresses, little time, pressure to perform and excel at your job, at home, various religions...there are plenty of temptations and distractions that can naturally distance you from your spiritual interactions with God.

And once you are off-course, The Enemy will only add more Temptations-Distractions and Complications in your life to reinforce his disconnection-grip on you...and away from true connectivity with God.

It's that simple!

You are just one target...

Imagine the very same thing happening to every person on earth...no time to think of God, or anyone else for that matter because you would be plunged into the physical world of surviving/making money/priorities/starting wars...reducing God into "having another chore you've got to do, He's in the back of your mind," or better yet: having no thoughts about God at all...

This is what The Enemy is counting on: Tempting, Distracting, and Complicating the world into a chaotic sense of being busy, without any regard for the spiritual...disconnected.

Ignorant Of Your Own Ignorance...And More

Here's something that The Enemy is counting on: you've been a victim of Satan's Weapons Of Total Chaos by simply not being aware of them!

Ignorance can and will be used against you by Satan to breed more Ignorance and distance you from God. You can then be molded and influenced by circumstances that can drift you further away from your Savior Jesus:

"They are darkened in their understanding and separated from the life of God because of the ignorance that is in them due to the hardening of their hearts (Ephesians 4:18, NIV)..."

In other words, The Destroyer distracts your mind away from understanding the real reasons for your discouragement, anger, bewilderment, vulnerability, confusion, hatred, jealousy, etc..by hardening your heart from understanding the reality of your personal relationship with God.

Once you've been kept in spiritual darkness with Ignorance, your supernatural blessings will be stripped from you; you will be weighed down with a flood of circumstances that would preoccupy your life and make your efforts getting back to God hard and time-consuming. Your struggle may last for years, in which case you might abandon every effort for a spiritual comeback because you don't feel like making the effort (Satan knows human nature: Laziness can drain any motivation to re-claim what you lost).

The real danger comes when you've been discouraged to a point where you convince your own mind that any further effort is useless; you may then develop an attitude of Indifference about your faith in God (that also affects your daily life)...even some anger against Him. You may still agree with Jesus and his Good News message of hope; but life's burdens may drag you down, making you feel too far gone from spiritual goals. You become weary and abandon any effort for a comeback:

"I am weary with my crying (Psalm 69:3, NAS)..."

"I am weary with my groaning (Psalm 6:6, KJV)..."

"My soul is weary of my life; I will leave my complaint upon myself; I will speak in the bitterness of my soul (Job 10:1, KJV)..."

The Deceiver is an expert in human nature; once you have been subjected to limited knowledge (Ignorance), too Lazy to find out more, and no longer caring to find out (Indifference), you will then fall into Forgetfulness which makes you totally vulnerable to any circumstance The Destroyer places in front of you. You won't remember how to defend supernaturally against disconnection from God; instead, you will seek answers where there is no anointing, no supernatural blessings, no bridging the gap between you and God.

At this stage, Satan's job is easy, but very effective: like a virus growing exponentially out of control, he lets you drown in your own helplessness, seeing yourself falling into circumstances that make your life spiritually empty, with no way out...And all because you have been de-sensitized in knowing that Ignorance, along with Laziness-Indifference and Forgetfulness have stripped you from the real potential: your incredible God-given power of communication!

Satan Orchestrates, But You Are Responsible For Your Actions

Maybe you are not directly to blame for not knowing about Satan's Weapons Of Total Chaos (because your parents never taught you the Word of God and Jesus, for example...). No matter, because at some point in your life, you do get to ask the question "what is this life all about?"

Besides (and let's not play naive), you do make conscious decisions as an adult; and depending on your actions and decisions, you will either raise yourself up higher, or stay stagnant...

The Enemy knows of your spiritual yearning for divine contact implanted in the depths of your being (have you ever wondered about life?); he will feed your spiritual sensitivities by sabotaging your spiritual journey *before* you even start, with Satan's Weapons Of Total Chaos.

Just like an athlete who prepares for competition, you need to prepare to run the good race of faith *by knowing your adversary's game-plan against you!*

This is why the apostle Paul stated in Hebrews 12:1-2 that you continue to 'run the good race of faith,' because Satan wants you to quit. The only reason you would ever stop is because you have either innocently or intentionally fallen into the trap of:

i) Ignorance, Laziness, Indifference, Forgetfulness;
ii) Assisted by Temptations, Distractions, Complications;
iii) And then pursued by a self-inflicted list of guilt trips, anger, helplessness, riches, power, discouragement, jealousy, etc...factors that cut off your communications with God.

God does not want you lose you, and has supplied the right conditions with simple instructions in the New Testament; but you need to understand that The Destroyer is aware of this, and will do everything to prevent you from reaching higher:

a) Satan knows what will set you off-course...
b) Using your natural vulnerabilities to steer you away from God...
c) Outside influences to blur your enthusiasm for God...
d) Use Satan's Weapons Of Total Chaos to disconnect you...
e) To keep you from the Key to your spiritual enablement: Jesus.

The Deceiver places great value in you because he knows that once you are naturally/spiritually contaminated by Ignorance-Laziness-Indifference-Forgetfulness, he will then use you to spread the contamination (knowingly and unknowingly) to others around you too, like a 'spiritual-virus.'

Satan Plants Seeds Too

Just like the parable in the Bible that compares your growing faith in God with the mustard seed (Matthew 13, 31-32):

"The kingdom of heaven is like a grain of mustard seed that a man took and sowed in his field. It is the smallest of all seeds, but when it has grown it is larger than all the garden plants and becomes a tree, so that the birds of the air come and make nests in its branches..."

The Destroyer also has his own "seeds" that can grow uncontrollably huge; only that his seeds will choke-off your spiritual contact with God.

And do you know the kind of "seeds" Satan plants?

You guessed it: Ignorance, Laziness, Indifference, and Forgetfulness...Satan's Weapons Of Total Chaos. Only that his "seeds" are meant to disconnect you from God. Along with Temptation, Distraction, and Complication to "water his seeds," Satan can make you become lost in a jungle of circumstances that can make you irretrievably lost in a twisted path of bad decisions and actions that is Sin.

Chapter 16

Sin

What is exactly this thing called Sin?

How is Sin defined in the dictionary?

In Meriam-Webster online, sin (noun) is defined as:

1) an offense against religious or moral law...
2a) a transgression of the law of God...
2b) a vitiated state of human nature in which **the self is estranged from God...**

Sin is all about cutting off your mindset to God...in other words, you lose contact with Him. But you are not alone; everyone sins, regardless if it is a thought, word or deed...no one is perfect:

"...for all have sinned and all short of the glory of God (Romans 3:23, NIV)..."

In matters of faith, sin is a major subject because it affects both your communications in the natural world, and your relationship with God.

It's a vicious circle: on the one hand, you want to get close to God, while on the other hand sin cuts you off...

Hiding behind the acts of sin is the real enemy that secretly infiltrates your life: Satan's Weapons Of Total Chaos...

Sin Is About Separation

God wants contact with you...He wants communication. But The Enemy does not share God's enthusiasm; he plans the opposite: to separate you from God.

Using Ignorance-Laziness-Indifference-Forgetfulness against you, Satan can alter your thinking, distancing any thoughts about God in your life; add circumstances that Tempt-Distract and Complicate...you end up being misled to making other decisions and actions (intentional or unintentional) that can completely cut off your communication to God.

And that's what sin is all about: **making decisions and taking actions that cause separation from God.**

Your Importance Has Been Recognized...by Satan

The Enemy knows:

a) that you are born to communicate;
b) the importance of your communication-relationship with God;

c) about Jesus, your Undisputed Champion and Savior;

d) Christ...your communications re-connector.

Your importance has been recognized by The Enemy, and wants to drive you into sinful acts and thoughts that will distance you from the Lord. These can be acts and thoughts of:

hate;

jealousy;

envy;

falsehood (lying, misleading, etc);

vengeance;

self-righteousness;

pride;

selfishness;

violence;

obsession;

doubt...etc.

But here's a surprise: The Deceiver can also separate you from God with *good thoughts and deeds* that distract your thinking; the Enemy doesn't care if you're enjoying success, as long as you haven't included God in the good things in your life!

And that in itself is also a sin (estranging yourself from God)!

Moreover, as a follower of Christ, The Enemy sees you differently: you are an ally with **Jesus who Satan could not defeat**, and he absolutely hates any alliance you may have with God's Undisputed Champion (Jesus)!

So Satan continues his campaign against you (and the rest of the world), by enticing you with Temptations-Distractions and Complications to alter your thinking and decision-making, leading you to acts of sin (ie. actions that estrange you from the Lord).

Sinful Acts

Understand how sin works in your life to help you avoid sinful acts because there is so much to lose both in the natural and spiritual universe once sin disconnects you from the Lord.

If your mindset is not "set on things above (Col. 3:2, NIV)," then any attempt to communicate in the spiritual has no way of being transmitted; you may have intentionally or unintentionally altered your communications away from God.

The Deceiver just needs to do a slight adjustment to your thinking, to alter how you communicate with your world; this will ultimately affect your actions which can disrupt your entire communication relationship with God. Anything that distracts your personal relationship with God is a disconnector, and is Sin...even a seemingly innocent thought or act can be considered a sin.

You can say that the word "sin" isn't only about lying or cheating or stealing...etc; it's anything that steers your thought away from God...

Action-Reaction Thinking

It is said that for every action there's also some kind of reaction. Good actions can bring good reactions, bad actions breed bad reactions; in God's world, your supernatural awakening is influenced by your thinking, and if your 'thinking-action' is not geared toward a relationship with God, then your 'thinking-reaction' will drive you away from Him:

"But I see in my members another law waging war against the law of my mind and making me captive to the law of sin that dwells in my members (Romans 7:23)."

If you are not mindful that God can help your daily challenges, and have decided that God has no room in your daily life, then you have decided that either you don't have time for God or that God has no time for you and your problems...

You could say that your mindset (your thinking) has been corrupted, infected, changed...estranged from God.

So if you are wondering why blessings and favor are not coming, maybe you should ask yourself: "have I left a place for God to reside in my heart, mind, and soul?" If not, your thinking can cause you to make decisions that will continue to separate you from a communication relationship with God.

It is all done starting with Satan's Weapons of Total Chaos...

Understand (and don't forget) that sin has no other purpose but to disrupt your natural/spiritual life and cut-off your communications to God, including any spiritual support from Him (blessings, favor, supernatural intervention in your life-circumstances, etc.)...

Hot or Cold

That's why in Revelation 3:15, Jesus says it like it is:

"...you are neither hot or cold. I wish you were either one or the other! (NIV)"

God doesn't want 'wishy-washy' thinking; you are either involving Him in your life or not, there is no in-between: you are either 'hot for God...or cold!'

Sometimes the proper conditions have not been set up for you:

1) example: parents not having taught you how to be with God when you were young, and grew up estranged from God;

2) example: a repressive society that restricts you in seeking out your faith-freedom in Christ;

3) Too frustrated (or no time) to be in contact with God;

4) You have no trust in God to intervene in your life...etc.

But there comes a time of personal reflection when your soul will be looking for some spiritual inspiration to break out of your spiritual limitations, seeking answers.

This is where Satan will find you at your most sensitive state, and drive you into an "action" that you think is right, but is not. So instead of producing a spiritual awakening, you are instead going through the motions of "playing some kind of religious ritual" but without any spiritual connection to God...

Taking You Off-Course...Slightly

(A little bit of science fact...)
Have you heard that altering the course of a space ship by even one degree can send it off-course by several thousand miles, even light-years (depending on distance)...?

The Enemy does the same thing with your attempt to communicate with God, altering (sometimes ever-so-slightly) your faith by using Satan's Weapons Of Total Chaos. Along with Temptation-Distraction and Complication, your life can go into tailspin of sinful acts, while your contact with God is cut off.

Realize this: by setting you spiritually off-course ever so slightly, Satan can keep you away from your contact with God by keeping you in Sin (disconnection). He does it by steering you away from Jesus, His redemption, and some key actions you need to take as a natural and spiritual person...

Your spiritual life can become lost in an endless maze as you try to find your way back to God; but without Jesus in the picture, you never do. You can be forever trapped in a spiritual whirlpool of separation (Sin) seeking answers and never finding them, drowning in a sea of religions and philosophies; and as entertaining as the other ideas and philosophies may be, you never find the keys to open doors to communication with the Creator Of The Universe.

Jesus explains it like this:

"A sower went out to sow his seed. And as he sowed, some fell along the path and was trampled underfoot, and the birds of the air devoured it. And some fell on the rock, and as it

105

grew up, it withered away, because it had no moisture. And some fell among the thorns, and the thorns grew up with it and choked it (Luke 8:5-7, ESV)..."

He goes on to explain:

"The seed is the word of God. The ones along the path are those who have heard; then the devil comes and takes away the word from their hearts, so that they may not believe and be saved. And the ones on the rock are those who, when they hear the word, receive it with joy. But these have no root; they believe for a while, and in time of testing fall away. And as for what fell among the thorns, they are those who hear, but as they go on their way they are choked by the cares and riches and pleasures of life, and their fruit does not mature (Luke 8:11-14, ESV)..."

You too may find yourself in circumstances, just like the seeds that are prevented to grow in harsh environments: you are prevented to spiritually grow and blossom as you should. Your environment may be causing a spiritual separation between yourself and God. Getting back may even seem impossible because your mind is constantly under fire from Ignorance-Laziness-Indifference-Forgetfulness, and assisted by the various Temptations, Distractions, and Complications of life itself...

In your mind, you may think it is next to impossible to restore full contact with God...

No worries: you will now find out how to overcome The Enemy, his Weapons of Total Chaos, and to restore the powerful potential of God's Word in your life...

106

PART TWO

THE SOLUTION:

(RESTORING COMMUNICATIONS)

Think on this for a moment:

"Do you realize that you've been **PRE-APPROVED** for re-entry in God's Winners' Circle?"

Yes it sounds funny; it's like saying you are pre-approved for a credit card, or a mortgage...

After all, what is the meaning of your life and all your abilities, if not to help you evolve to a higher purpose?

Your natural world is just a stepping-stone, a personal journey into a greater understanding of your purpose with the One who has granted you this incredible life...

You're even made to wonder about your life: haven't you ever thought to yourself, "what is my life all about," or "what is the meaning of my life?"

Look, you were NOT put on this earth just to pay bills, work for a living, and then die...you've been pre-approved to reach a higher level, a spiritual one, and celebrate your life together with God!

Question: can you grow in spiritual contact with The Creator by:

1. Keeping yourself Ignorant?
2. Lazy to find out more?
3. Indifferent?
4. Forgetful of the spiritual?
5. Be a victim Temptation, Distraction and Complication?
6. Be forever trapped in the natural world?
7. Follow 'feel-good only' philosophies?
8. Complicate any sense of faith with rules, procedures and other complications?

Answer: No, they weaken your mind, and separate you from the Lord.

You want the opposite:

1. uncomplicate what has been complicated;
2. restore your pre-approved ability to communicate with God;
3. renew your pre-approved loving relationship with God;
4. release pre-approved blessings and favor intended for you...

In other words, you want to save youself from your own:

a. lack of understanding that you are pre-approved to reach God;
b. Ignorance, Laziness, Indifference, and Forgetfulness and:
c. fall from Temptations, Distractions and Complications...

Understand that God was always interested in your communications contact with Himself and has implanted within you the seeds of pre-approval to join Him in His eternal community.

"REFER TO THE MANUAL"

Have you ever thought of the Bible as an "instruction manual?"

It's time you did!

The chapters of the Old and New Testament are not just nice stories; they are instructions that restore your unification and pre-approval to God.

And what are these instructions? Solutions to Ignorance-Laziness-Indifference and Forgetfulness, igniting the divine intervention of God's love in your natural and spiritual life, and guiding you to a joyful relationship with the Father...

And the instructions are so lovely, inspiring...and easy to read!

Amazingly, Jesus' instructions of spiritual reconciliation, his deeds of love, non-violence, and compassion are being misunderstood: attacked, ignored, set aside, manipulated, forgotten, and even persecuted. This leaves the door wide open for spiritual corruption and a deepening of Ignorance-Laziness-Indifference-Forgetfulness in both the spiritual and natural life!

And that's what The Enemy wants: total communications blackout in the spiritual battlefield...

(NOW PLEASE READ THE NEXT PARAGRAPH CAREFULLY)

"The Word of God can never be extinguished. The Enemy's objective is to extinguish the Word FROM YOU!"

Remember, Satan failed in his chance to defeat Jesus' mission on earth and prevent the resulting surge which became Christianity...

So what does The Deceiver do? He attacks the next closest thing that God loves: YOU AND THE REST OF THE WORLD by planting the seeds of Ignorance-Laziness-Indifference-Forgetfulness to cut off your communications from God and prevent you from ever reconciling with His Undefeated Champion Jesus; to never find out that you are pre-approved!

Jesus clearly knew of Satan's intentions, and spoke about it to his unsuspecting opponents:

"You belong to your father, the devil...He was a murderer from the beginning, not holding to the truth, for there is no truth in him...for he is a liar and the father of lies (John 8:44 NIV)."

A NEW SURGE

So what have you found out so far?

1. You were born to communicate;
2. A victim of Satan's Weapons Of Total Chaos...

And now, a new realization:

YOU ARE PRE-APPROVED for re-unification with God!

It should build in you a new surge of interest, a renewed curiosity for learning how to restore and enjoy your communications with Him. With Satan's "soft underbelly" exposed, you can have a clear advantage over him, with a renewed understanding that you have:

"...the authority to trample on snakes and scorpions and to overcome all the power of the enemy; nothing will harm you (Luke 10:19, NIV)..."

It means that you are pre-approved to overcome all obstacles.

The term "surge" means a building-up of a powerful thrust; by knowing that you are pre-approved to enter God's kingdom, you can now "thrust forward" with a renewed surge of desire to re-align your understanding of your relationship with God in your life, and in your circumstances.

So here is the first surge that will thrust you in the direction of restoring communications with God:

Believe God loves you, as a Father, as a friend, as:

"...Abraham believed God, and it was credited to him as righteousness, and he was called God's friend (James 2:23)."

Abraham's relationship with God was so personal and spiritually intentional, that he was recognized as God's friend.

Imagine: God's friend!

It means that Abraham related to God as if He was right there with him, sharing his experiences with the Lord...his pleasure, his pain, his circumstances; and the Lord encouraged Abraham, dispensing supernatural help throughout his life journey...

Isn't that what friends do, love one another and give help when needed?

Abraham consciously and intentionally opened his heart to God because he was interested in a loving and meaningful communications relationship with Him...He loved to include God's presence in his daily life!

So, your first surge into re-establishing communications with God is:

You are pre-approved for unification with God, and:

Believe God loves you (like Abraham)..."

Next, how do you get to believe God on such a deep and personal level where you too can be credited as being righteous to be called God's friend?

You prepare your whole self to step into 'God's Winners' Circle...'

Chapter 17

Expecting The Unexpected

Have you ever felt the excitement of having understood something that you hadn't before? Something that seemed incomprehensible and, unexpectedly, it all came together in your mind and you finally made sense of it?

God's Winners' Circle is all about receiving unexpected levels of life-changing experiences that were pre-approved by God all along!

The KEY is to re-position your mind to understand that you are pre-approved; knowing this, your thinking patterns change: you re-position your heart, mind, soul, and spirit to welcome God's love into your life unconditionally (just as if you give unconditional love to someone you care for: your wife, your husband, your children...etc). Suddenly, with God's inspirational touch, your spiritual eyes will open unexpectedly; you will start to see more clearly, with a new-found desire to get closer to God...

You get the "Oh yeah! Now I get it!" moment...

Your zest of life is re-ignited, as your soul soars toward the spiritual, expecting more wisdom to arrive unexpectedly, anticipating a better understanding of His Word and His intentions. It will instantly excite you to welcome God in your life even more as you witness a new warmth of His lovingkindness filling up your heart:

"For by grace you have been saved through faith. And this is not your own doing; it is the gift of God (Ephesians 2:8, ESV);"

"Every good gift and every perfect gift is from above, coming down from the Father of lights (James 1:17, ESV);"

"If any of you lacks wisdom, let him ask God, who gives generously to all without reproach, and it will be given to him (James 1:5, ESV)."

His presence in you grows as you begin to sense a mysterious spiritual re-alignment as never before.

Longing, Desiring

Entering God's Winners' Circle is no small thing; you need to intentionally re-tune your mind to understand that you are pre-approved to enter into an area of great privilege, reserved for those who:

"long to dwell in His tent (Ps. 61:4);"
"where God is your fortress (Ps. 62:2);"
"filled with the good things of God's house (Ps. 65:4)."

Notice the words "long to dwell," "God is your fortress," and "filled with the good things..."

114

They communicate some kind of hopeful expectation:

a) wanting to belong to Him ("long to dwell");
b) expecting His safety and security ("God is your fortress");
c) receiving the good things in life ("love, peace, prosperity...").

So think on this for a moment:

-Do you long to dwell in God's tent?
-Do you desire Him to be your ever-present, guardian (fortress)?
-Do you wait for Him to fill your life with goodness?

The key here is hopeful expectation (longing, desiring, waiting)...

If you desire to dwell in God's house, and you desire to enjoy His supernatural security and the good things He has intended for you, then you must do your part: invite Him into your heart, re-position yourself to hope and:

1. **expect** new supernatural wisdom (not Ignorance);
2. **expect** to be spiritually energized (not Lazy);
3. **expect** renewed interest in the spiritual (not Indifferent);
4. **expecting** to maintain a fresh new standard (not Forgetful).

You are purposely adjusting your heart, welcoming the heartfelt hope of divine communication. God will sense your honest expectations for contact; and He will unexpectedly open new doors of understanding to encourage your mind to pursue full entry into God's Winners' Circle.

You will come to understand and expect that:

a) God is with you all the time, 24/7;

    i) He is no part-time God;

    ii) No genie-in-a-bottle;

    iii) Not around on your 'time-schedule' only;

    iv) He's here, all the time, through your good times and bad;

    v) He sees all your decisions and actions;

    vi) Nothing is hidden from Him:

       "what you have said in the dark will be heard in the daylight...(Luke 12:3);"

    vii) And He is always accessible:

       "And behold, I am with you always, to the end of the age (Matthew 28:20, ESV)."

b) Personalize your relationship with God.

As you welcome Him into your hopeful heart, believe and expect:

- no more barriers between you and God;
- communication with God on a personal level, one-on-one;
- to receive blessings and favor custom fit for you;
- a relationship with child-like faith and heartfelt gratitude, a father-to-child relationship and not 'that He owes you.'

c) God too expects.

As you understand that you are pre-approved, The Creator of Everything expects genuine contact from you, communications of heartfelt love, without formalities...enjoying Him in your life...

Have you ever considered talking to God casually, in a heartfelt one-on-one, confiding in Him as you would with a friend (wife, brother/sister, pastor, etc.) with whom you have a close connection?

You should...He expects it!

He gave you the power to communicate so that you can reach out to Him too!

How do you talk to God?

Relate it to your real-life experience: Do you ever talk to someone you love in a formal, stiff, business-like manner? Or do you speak casually, friendly, with interest and genuine respect?

So why should your conversation be any different with God?

Jesus showed the complicated and distorted world how to communicate with God through His own actions: throughout the New Testament, He spoke to God with respectful, heartfelt interest...just as He would talk to someone on earth.

So do what Jesus did: speak with heartfelt expectation that God listens to you...because He does!

d) Personalize, Personalize, Personalize...

Put yourself in a "first person" prayer-communication position with Him; this means that when you read a verse from the Bible, personalize the verse for yourself. Relate God's message to you, as if He custom-wrote the verse only for you...so take it and personalize it in your heart!

For example, when you read "The Lord protects the pure of heart..." meditate on the message, don't hurry, personalize the phrase within your heart, saying with humility and gratitude:

"Lord I believe and trust that you protect the purity of my heart..."

Here is another example: "He shields us from danger..." can be personalized:

"You shield me from danger..."

The Word is meant to stir your heart into a loving spiritual communication with God; so help engage your heart to The Word by doing this: read The Word in the Bible as if it were written personally for you. Open your heart to its lovingkindness, and then express it in your own loving words, speaking it into your life.

Remember: The Word are instructions to help bring forth heartfelt communication; you are engaging in a faith that is alive and intensely personal. Invite the message of Christ to engage into your life, and communicate intimately, respectfully with God...as you would do with those you really love (your spouse, your children, your parents, for example).

e) Expect that you will receive His blessings and favor.

Make God's Word your Word.

Not because you have to...not because you must...or forced.

Do so because it makes perfect sense to your evolving spiritual mindset. You no longer want to be Ignorant-Lazy-Indifferent-Forgetful...a victim of Satan Weapons Of Total Chaos. You want to be a vibrant, natural-spiritual person, pre-approved by The Lord, reaching out and tapping into your new-found understanding behind the incredible power of your communication...using it lovingly and unconditionally.

Open your heart to expect both His love and His compassion, just as the story in the Bible of the blind men who opened their heart to Jesus (Matthew 9:28-30) in the hope of regaining their ability to see:

"Do you believe that I am able to do this? Yes Lord," they replied...and their sight was restored..."

They invited the love of God in their hearts and hoped for miraculous healing...which they unexpectedly received.

f) Your greatest key to your expectations is Jesus.

Let's talk about Jesus...

Every Christian's journey to the Lord is different, but Christ is the common denominator; He is the "master key" that guides your spirit to rise and reach out to God. With Jesus as your mentor, He reminds that you are pre-approved for supernatural connection...that you are important to God. His mentoring helps you regain and restore your communication link with God in a spiritually intimate relationship, a Father-to-son/daughter-like bond...not a master/slave mentality as some other religions preach...

Imagine, you are both pre-approved AND have your own personal saviour (Jesus) to help open (or re-open) your spiritual communications back with God!

But Why Jesus?

What is so special about Jesus?

Forget everything for a moment, and consider this:

"Why is Jesus so important as 'The One' who will restore your communication-relationship with God over anyone else?"

Because He bridged the gap between humanity and God, reconciling The Creator with His creation (you) in a Father-to child mentality, and expect salvation as one who is pre-approved:

"For the Son of Man has come to seek and to save that which is lost (Luke 19:10, NASB)..."

"...that Christ Jesus came into the world to save (Timothy 1:15, NASB)..."

"And there is no salvation in no one else; for there is no other name under heaven that has been given among by which we must be saved (Acts 4:12, NASB)..."

Jesus has released you from the original sin that drove the original man and woman (Adam and Eve) into the curse of separation from God...

120

Separation came in the form of...disobedience:

And The Lord commanded the man saying, "You may surely eat of every tree in the garden, but of the tree of the knowledge of good and evil you shall not eat, for in the day that you eat of it you shall surely die (Genesis 2:16-17, ESV)..."

As the scriptures reveal, Adam and Eve fell into the Temptation to eat the forbidden fruit:

"Have you eaten from the tree of which I commanded you not to eat? (Genesis 3:11, ESV)..."

Whether it was done innocently or on purpose, God's message became clear: disobedience brought unexpected destabilization and separation from Himself...

And then came the consequences:

"...through painful toil you will eat food from it all the days of your life (Genesis 3:17, NIV)..."

"By the sweat of your brow you will eat your food until you return to the ground (Genesis 3:19, NIV)..."

"So the Lord God banished him from the Garden Of Eden to work the ground from which he had been taken (Genesis 3:19, NIV)..."

And this remains to this day: separation brings hardship, sweat, toil, and banishment from the bliss that the original man and woman first enjoyed; sadly, this disconnection has since been passed on from generation to generation...

But it is not permanent!

Great News: Reconciliation Is Here

Jesus goes where no other has gone before: he reconciles you back to God; He shares the Great News that expectations of reconciliation to Father God is possible, through a personal and intimate relationship with Him...a Father-to-child interaction.

Jesus becomes God's voice on earth, the contact-point from which you begin your revival; His mentorship teaches you that it is never too late to expect God to enter your life once again and enjoy an unexpected relationship with Him in the physical world...

And what is this unexpected relationship? It's a love-relationship based on genuine trust that unexpected supernatural blessings will help re-align your heart and mind. It comes through a renewed interest in reaching out to the Lord, admitting that you need (and welcome) His presence in your life.

Reaching out to someone for the warmth of compassion and understanding is not new to you (example: reaching out to your husband/wife, parents, friends...); do the same with God: reach out to Him!

The divine invitation is already there to claim for your own...

God's Love...For You

Have you ever felt an inner warmth knowing that someone out

there really loves you? It may be your wife, your husband, your children, your parents, your friends, acquaintances...? It stirs up your emotions in various ways: you feel an anticipation that something good exists in your life; sensing a knowing that you are considered important, that you matter to someone.

That you are loved...

The world suddenly looks like a better place; you look at people with fondness, and life just simply feels great. You like doing nice things to people; and people like to do nice things for you, even if it is just saying a casual hello...

It's all based on the emotion of love: love is the emotional bond that brings everything together. It brings calm, it overcomes any obstacle and any other emotion because love is a unifier, not a separator; it is an emotion that in it's purest form, unconditional:

"Love does no harm to its neighbour (Romans 13:10, NIV)..."

"Love is patient, love is kind. It does not envy, it does not boast, it is not proud. It is not rude, it is not self-seeking, it is not easily angered. It keeps no record of wrongs. Love does not delight in evil but rejoices with the truth...Love never fails (1 Corinthians 13:4-8, NIV)..."

Love works the same way in the spiritual: when you realize that you've been pre-approved to reunite with a loving God, you can't help sensing that you are loved; it motivates you to draw closer to Him, expecting somehow that His Love will not let you down...

Associate it with your natural life: for example, wouldn't you draw closer to someone who loves you, like your mother, father, brother, sister, friend, pet...so why not do the same with the Creator of all existence? Draw close to Him too!

Love is an action-packed emotion: it is a feeling you can transmit to someone, a signal of expected intimacy, for drawing closer, and a chance for communication:

"Dear children, let us not love with words or tongue but with actions and in truth (1 John 3:18, NIV)..."

Love is never on the defensive: it is an active, giving emotion that brings out the best in you. This is especially true when you know that someone really loves you: wouldn't you offer the best of yourself to that person? It is a normal expectation...

In the atmosphere of suspicion and suppression of His time, Christ's message of this expecting reconciliation with God through love was an eye-opener; and his message is just as important today.

After all, giving true love is a free, natural, powerful, yet unconditional expression of communication you can transmit to anyone. Christ had mentioned it in the Bible:

"Greater love has no one than this: to lay down one's life for one's friends (John 15:13, NIV)..."

And the more unconditional love you show to others, the more you can understand God's Love for you, and the greater your appreciation for everything in your life that is good and noble.

By opening your longing heart to God's Love, you are inviting divine communication; welcoming a loving God into your own loving heart can bring unexpected blessings and favored changes in your life, and you will know that it is from God's Hand:

"Blessed be the Lord, who daily bears us up (Ps. 68:19, ESV);"

"For the Lord God is a sun and shield; the Lord bestows favor and honor. No good thing does he withhold from those who walk uprightly (Ps.84:11, ESV);"

"Therefore do not be anxious saying "What shall we eat? or What shall we drink...seek first the kingdom of God and his righteousness, and all these things will be added to you (Matthew 6:31-33, ESV)."

Notice the words: "He bears us up...God is a sun and shield...all these things will be added to you..."

By now you have realized that 'someone up there' loves you; with this in mind, extend your loving heart and make spiritual contact with God, knowing that He has already pre-approved you to enter into His Freedom Circle. You are loved and not abandoned...

Imagine the growing sense of euphoria when you understand that God has always loved you...and maybe a bit disappointed that you hadn't realized it until now.

No matter; today is the beginning of great days ahead...

Start expecting God to come into your life; lovingly reach out to Him, signalling that you want interaction with Him, that your spirit needs a relationship with Him. No more being in the dark (Ignorant), unmotivated (Lazy), not interested (Indifferent), and unmindful (Forgetful)...

You are ready to claim your spot in God's Winners' Circle!

Chapter 18

With God, Intentionally

You're starting to understand that God had already implanted in you the seeds of a champion; you've been His **pre-approved** spiritual winner all along, but never realized it!

The Enemy, Satan, diverted your mindset from having any realization of this genuine quality in you; Ignorance, Laziness, Indifference, and Forgetfulness have played a key role in depriving you the right to claim your spot in God's Winners' Circle.

But now you know better...

NOTICE: Staying in contact with God does not mean your responsibilities and challenges in life will disappear; you still have bills to pay, a family to raise, a career to build, responsibility at work, doing the chores at home, etc. But with this new knowledge, you can better handle your battles in your favor with God's help.

"Yeah but I still get frustrated with all that I've got to do," you might say.

Being spiritual won't make your responsibilities and emotions disappear, but take note:

Your responsibilities and eathly experiences become even MORE important than you think: they become real life exercises to help solidify your re-unification with The Creator Of All Existence.

Suddenly all the things that you do on earth have a SPECIAL ROLE to play in both your natural AND spiritual progress (more on this later)!

And the key to your successful achievement toward a balanced natural and spiritual life has to do with your OWN WILLINGESS to communicate with God for everything that you do!

In God's Winners' Circle...Intentionally

Have you ever done things in your life intentionally? Of course you have, practically all the time. For example:

a. Pursued an education;
b. Built a career, or changed it for a new one;
c. Formed a relationship with someone;
d Landscaped your back yard just the way you wanted;
e. Bought your favorite car;
f. Played sports...etc.
g. Woke up, got yourself out of bed, etc!

"Intentionally" means that you are doing something on purpose, exercising a voluntary action because you want to...

What if you had the same intentions toward God, wanted to invite Him into your life intentionally because you want to?

127

Your own willful intentions will help you to:

1. re-align your interest to re-unite with God;
2. get motivated to look deeper and make contact;
3. build your interest to actively pursue communication with Him;
4. intentionally mindful that you are **pre-approved** by God.

This isn't some ritual hocus-pocus; your desire for contact is a personal yearning from your soul to reach out to the spiritual world. And the more your willful intention for contact with The Creator of Everything, the more your soul will want to reach out...

Just as Jesus said in Luke 10:27:

"Love the Lord your God with all your heart and with all your soul and with all your strength and with all your mind..."

When you love someone, you try to involve them in your daily life as much as possible, right? Imagine welcoming God in your heart, involving Him in your life: your work, your play, your sleep, your listening to music, your sports, your video-games, your relationship with others...etc? You are showing **intentional** and sincere acceptance of His presence in everything you do...just as you intentionally do with those you love right now (wife/husband, kids, friends, relatives, associates, co-workers, your pets...etc)!

Do you see it?

If you've made sense of this association, then you've opened an uncontainable opportunity in you to expand into the supernatural side...God's side. Remember you are PRE-APPROVED to lovingly and intentionally welcome God into your life because of his infinite Love for you:

128

1) you've already been **pre-approved** for reconciliation;
2) born to communicate on a physical and **spiritual** level;
3) God seeks your **intentional** re-unification;
4) intentional reconciliation with genuine, **unconditional Love**...

The more you realize that you are "pre-approved for reconciliation with God on a physical and spiritual level by communicating intentional, unconditional love..." the greater your desire to change your life and make it more 'in-tune' with The Lord.

Wouldn't you change your life in order to accommodate someone you love and respect (your spouse, a friend, an associate..)?

You can't help but wanting to make some personal changes for a relationship to work...well, it's no different with God!

Good Intentions Over Confusion

Your desire to join God and His Winners' Circle becomes so powerful, that just a little bit of your intentional effort to let Him in your heart will start re-aligning your life toward the better, clearing your way through any confusion in your life-journey...

Imagine what happens when you really get into it...imagine the blessings God sends your way!

Your success depends on how far you will go to understand:

1. Your incredible power of your communications;
2. Ignorance-Laziness-Indifference-Forgetfulness;
3. How Temptations, Distractions, and Complications work;
4. Knowing yourself as a natural AND spiritual person;

5. You are pre-approved;
6. Your ability to communicate spiritually with **intention**;
7. That God wants your unconditional love for Him...

Restoring The Power Of The Word...In You Intentionally

You've been hearing much about 'God's Word' and 'God's Will' in faith-discussions and church sermons...

Especially about 'God's Word.'

What is 'God's Word' in the Bible all about?

Think on this:

What does "Word" mean?

It's a verbal signal, an interaction...it is communication.

So what do you do with a 'word...?'

You communicate with it.

So what does "God's Word" do then?

It communicates a message, in this case it enables (or in many cases, restores) spiritual interaction with Him!

God's Word in Christ takes it a step further: it helps you enter the spiritual world by showing you how to freely COMMUNICATE YOUR OWN SPIRITUAL TOOL: the love in your heart communicated intentionally, willingly, and unconditionally...an expression of pure, genuine love!

The Word enables you to communicate closer to God who has already pre-approved you.

Sure, you may have plenty of complex issues (example: the kids need shoes, the mortgage/rent is due, your marriage is stressed, the roof needs to be replaced, etc.)...and they preoccupy your time. Your major challenge is **remembering** to bring balance to your natural life with the spiritual (remember Forgetfulness?)...

You may even be tempted to think that the spiritual has nothing to do with your natural life with all its circumstances, and driven to **not caring** about spiritual pursuits (remember Indifference?)...

That's why Jesus is so important: Jesus is "God's Word in human form" that brings together what Satan is trying to separate: living a natural and supernatural life that is blended and balanced together under the protective umbrella of Love.

So Christ is the human demonstration of this natural and supernatural life blended together...He is The Word. He is **RECONCILIATION**; Christ is "the message:" that God wants contact, and He has already provided you the tools to do so.

And what are these 'tools?'

1) Your intentional awareness that you are pre-approved for reconciliation;
2) Your God-given ability to communicate on both the natural and spiritual level;
3) your true intentions, and your unconditional love!

Jesus is your activator, your guide for reunification:

"In the beginning was the Word, and the Word was with God, and the Word was God. He was with God in the beginning (John 1:1,2, NIV)..." and:

"The Word became flesh and made his dwelling among us..." (John 1:14, NIV)...

You Can Do This...Intentionally

Once you understand that Jesus is God's Word in human form, then Satan's Weapons Of Total Chaos will find it increasingly difficult to separate your mindset away from the Lord with negative thinking such as:

1. God has let you down;
2. God cannot be trusted;
3. He doesn't understand you;
4. He is at fault for your misfortunes;
5. He isn't doing enough to protect you;
6. Your relationship with God isn't going exactly as you planned it;
7. God hasn't helped you yet;
8. You are not good enough for His attention;
9. You are not strong, smart, or wise enough for His blessings...

The great news is that your road to reconciliation with God was pre-approved even before you were born!

You also have the built-in ability to **intentionally** re-align your mind, soul, and spirit; so instead of complaining and venting your frustrations for a life not yet fullfilled, send out an intentional signal to God that your heart is open to welcome Him into your life, just as Jesus coached you to do. Then watch yourself transform!

What a winning combination: God in heaven, and Jesus on earth!

But you may have a problem: you don't know where or how to start feeling the Word as a living part of your communication life! Yes, you pray, and ask for favor...yet you are not sure if you are really reaching out, or are simply "going through feel-good rituals" that amount to nothing.

HOW TO START

(Realize this right now: you have the tools to make your reconciliation with God real and intentional...you were born with them!)

Here's how to start:

1) Remind yourself (and believe) that God approves of you...
2) Make yourself accessible to God by welcoming Him with genuine anticipation and expectation...
3) Invite His contact with heartfelt Love.

But how can you reach out to God with Love? How do you transmit heartfelt Love to someone you can't see?

Do it as you do with the people you love here on earth. Try it now:

i)   Choose someone you love unconditionally (spouse, parents, sister, kids, friends, etc)? Do you desire their company?

ii)   Do you make the effort to please them because they are an important part of your life?

iii)   Do you go out of your way to help them the best way you can because you really care for their well-being?

iv)   You wouldn't do anything to intentionally hurt them?

v)   Do you feel that "warm and fuzzy feeling" when you are close to them, even when there is nothing to say?

vi)   Grateful for having them in your life?

vii)   They count on your good intentions, and you won't let them down...?

Well, do the same with God (use the same points above):

a) Do you love Him unconditionally and desire to be with Him intentionally, because you enjoy His company?

b) Do you make the effort to please Him because God is an important part of your life?

c) Do you go out of your way to stay close to God because you really care for your relationship with Him?

d) You wouldn't do anything to hurt Him?

e) Do you feel that spiritual "warm and fuzzy feeling" when you sense His presence, even when there is nothing to say?

f) Grateful for having Him in your life?

g) He can count on your good intentions...?

Do you see the emotional associations? Check them out:

Unconditional love and belonging;

Making the effort to please;
Caring relationship;
Not hurting;
The warm and fuzzy feeling of togetherness;
Grateful;
Never let them down...

You may not see this, but God has given you a clue here: Reach out to Him the same way you reach out to those you sincerely and unconditionally love here on earth. God has implanted in you the emotional need to bond with other people, to communicate; use the very same ability to connect with Him, with sincerity and good intention.

And now, you have the ability to do so because:

Christ shows you how!

Jesus hasn't really invented anything new; God has already implanted in you the answer to reconciliation. Jesus simply reveals something you already knew but was buried from your realization through Ignorance-Laziness-Indifference and Forgetfulness.

Even though it was mentioned in the previous chapter, it merits to remind you once more: the central element to restoring communication-contact with God, or with your world, is Love:

"Love is patient, love is kind. It does not envy, it does not boast, it is not proud. it does not dishonor others, it is not self-seeking, it is not easily angered, it keeps no record of wrongs. Love does not delight in evil but rejoices with the truth. It always protects, always trusts, always hopes, always perseveres (1 Corinthians 13:4-7, NIV)."

Do you see the association? Love releases intentional expressions of heartfelt communication, a longing and keen interest for someone in your life. It's a trusting act of personal interaction.

Now imagine having the same personal relationship with God...it's awesome! You can talk to Him about anything!

Reach Out Intentionally...To Him

God wants you to demonstrate your willingness and loyalty to Him, that you are intentionally reaching out and waiting for Him to show up in your life.

As you have just read, life itself provides you with real-life experiences that you can associate with your relationship with God:

Just as you put an effort to maintain a relationship with your spouse;
Just as you dedicate yourself to your career;
Just as you care for your family's well-being;
Just as you maintain your relationship with your best friend...

You must seek God with:

1. Intentional effort;
2. Dedication;
3. Caring;
4. A maintained relationship...

As soon as you have felt a keen interest for intentional contact with God, your next step is: how do you solidify this special relationship?

You revive yourself to Him...

Chapter19

Revived With God

Have you ever been in a special relationship?

When you like someone (for example), do you see that person differently, with greater interest, allowing that person closer to your heart? You suddenly feel that your life has greater meaning, doesn't it? It feels that you are connected to that person; you feel rejuvinated, renewed, satisfied...revived!

Or, do you recall accomplishing something (example: landed a new job, graduated from college, got a promotion, finished building the shed, redecorated your bedroom, etc): you sense an emotional uplifting; don't you feel enlightened, accomplished, revived...?

There are thousands of examples of big and small accomplishments; all provide the same result: the feeling of being revived!

Revival with God is exactly the same; it's another form of accomplishment: transmitting a genuine and honest sense of reconciliation that overwhelms your heart and your mind. You feel your restoration with God: a rekindling of a loving relationship that

He always wanted (and expected) from you!

And God is ready to provide what you need for your revival:

"For I know the plans I have for you, declares the Lord, plans for welfare and not for evil, to give you a future and a hope (Jeremiah 29:11, ESV)..." and:

"Come to me, all who labor and are heavy laden, and I will give you rest (Matthew 11:28, ESV)..." and:

"Call to me and I will answer you, and will tell you great and hidden things that you have not known (Jeremiah 33:3, ESV)..."

God expects your communication; He's already reserved a place for you in God's Winners' Circle...you just have to reach out for it!

This pre-approved victory should revive your inner senses to pursue an outstanding relationship with God. It's a relationship that He wants with you...a living spiritual relationship that is based on Love:

"Anyone who does not love does not know God, because God is love (1 John 4:8, ESV)."

Have you ever experienced love in your life?

Love seems to be a mystical, binding force; it should be no surprise to you then that it is also the common denominator for re-igniting your communication with God. It isn't enough to accumulate all the knowledge and wealth of the universe; you also need the binding force that launches you to the higher level, which is Love:

"If I have the gift of prophecy and can fathom all the mysteries and all knowledge, and if I have faith that can move mountains, *but do not have love*, I am nothing (1 Corinthians 13:2, NIV)."

Remember that God loved you first, and as a patient Father, He waits for you to make the intentional move back to Him with love:

"We love because he first loved us (1 John 4:19, NIV)."

God was there with you always...even now He waits to sense your reviving desire to be with Him...

Keeping Your Faith "Alive"

Whatever your circumstances, God wants to be involved in your life:

in your career;
in your leisure;
in your family;
in your sleep;
in your boredom;
in your problems;
in your excitement;
in your finances;
in your personal development;
in all that you do..!

God wants to FEEL your revived desire for contact with Him. He does not want to be "only for Sunday, on the sidelines, the last thing on your agenda," or daily "to-do" routine...going through the motions without meaning. Just as you feel a meaningfully-revived love for the people who are close to you, God wants to sense your living love for Him too:

To desire His presence (Ask);
To find Him (Seek);
To call on Him (Knock) (ref: Matthew 7:7)

The clues lie within your heart: are you letting God get involved in your life because you want Him intentionally in it?

His Word, Your Life

Many folks go to church, know the scriptures word-for-word...but do they actually live those words in their daily lives? Are they revived to motivate themselves to the next level of faith, or are they merely reading the words because they 'make them feel good' in their sorrow?

In other words, is the Word "intentionally alive" in them?

And what about you:

1. You understand you can communicate with God one-on one?
2. That Satan's Weapons of Total Chaos hold back your blessings?
3. That you are Tempted to be Distracted into Complications?
4. You are pre-approved to interact with God from the start?
5. Believe that God loves you?
6. Are you open to expect to receive blessings and favor?
7. You keenly interested in an intentional relationship with God?
8. Are you seeking to revive your relationship with Him?

If you have grasped the understanding of these, then you can't help sensing a desire to revive intentionally with God; your heart welcomes His Mind, His thoughts, His Will, His Word...in other words you are trying to communicate with Him because you WANT to be in the company of the loving Lord!

You WANT to feel your relationship with God as you do with your wife, your husband, your child, your best friend: to feel a vibrancy inside you, a warm companionship reviving in your heart.

And you know what? God expects you to take those emotions He's planted in you and use them to reach out to Him!

Your emotions are not meant only to desire a big house, a fast car, lots of money, etc. The Creator implanted these feelings so you can use them both in your natural world, and channel it out to Him!

Just as you feel that there is someone there for you in the natural world, reach out to sense the secure companionship in the spiritual too!

Just as in the parable of the Prodigal Son (Luke 15:11-32), about a wayward son returning to his father, God wants to see you come back home to Him...voluntarily and with genuine, honest longing for Himself. And as a father is happy to welcome back his lost child, the Lord will want to do the same for you once He senses your genuine desire to reach out to Him:

"I will set out and go back to my father and say to him: Father I have sinned against heaven and against you (Luke 15:18, NIV)..."

You'd be surprised on how loving God can be toward you; He will sense your genuine heart seeking Him out, and He will come to you:

"But while he was still a long way off, his father saw him and was filled with compassion for him; he ran to his son, threw his arms around him and kissed him. The son said to him, 'Father, I have sinned against heaven and against you. I am no longer worthy to be called your son.' But the father said to his servants 'Quick! Bring the best robe and put it on him. Put a ring on his finger and sandals on his feet. bring the fattened calf and kill it. Let's have a feast and celebrate. For this son of mine was dead and is alive again; he was lost and is found. So they began to celebrate (Luke 15:20-24, NIV)..."

Have you ever had a similar reunion with someone special (a brother, a parent, a cousin, an old friend...) that you haven't spoke to (or even seen) for a long time? If you have, do you remember the joy of that moment of reconciliation?

Just like the Parable Of The Prodigal Son, God is right here, waiting to see you in the distance coming back to Him; He knows that you are reaching out in heartfelt longing to re-connect...to revive your relationship with Him.

And He will do the same...

This is intentional communication: your genuine spiritual yearning, wanting to call out to the Lord with a newly-revived heartfelt love that can restore your relationship with Him...

This is no hocus-pocus magic trick or some artificial need...your emotional need for spiritual re-contact is implanted in you to

142

establish and maintain a relationship in both the natural and spiritual world.

But it is up to you to channel your desire to reunite with God...The Lord awaits your heartfelt communication!

Recognize Separation

Of course Satan's Weapons Of Total Chaos will always be there too, 24/7, to ensure that you remain separate, unrevived from the Word of God. Through years of Ignorance-Laziness-Indifference-Forgetfulness, and followed by Temptations-Distractions-Complications, you can remain separated from God by:

-not understanding your own power of communication;
-not confident of your ability to speak with the Lord;
-not wanting to be forced into the Word;
-not knowing how to get back to God;
-not exactly sure what heartfelt intention is;
-expecting nothing;
-not deserving God's favor;
-remaining unrevived...

It must appear to you a daunting task to turn to God for help, especially when your attention is concentrating on everything else EXCEPT God...

The good news is that returning to God isn't hard...

Just recognize that whatever the distractions, they are meant to separate you from contact with God and His divine blessings!

Take your lessons from life: when you sense a conflict, don't you spend some time and energy to deal with it?

Do the same with God: you must want God to come into your life; asking, seeking, knocking on the door (Matthew 7:7), earnestly wanting God to enter in your daily life.

Speak your defense (example): "Lord, I know that the Enemy is trying to separate me from the relationship I have with you by using my... (any difficult situation: your own ego, jealousy, debt, addiction, some wrongdoing by someone...etc); but I stand steadfast Lord, humbly cuddling in your Embrace, pre-approved to communicate with you, residing in Your House in The Spirit, that good things shall come to pass as I continue to celebrate my relationhsip with you in both body and soul. I release my situation to you. Just help me to remain patient Lord as I gaze up to you in expectation for your guidance as I endure this problem..."

Just as you hold onto your relationship with your spouse, your kids, your friends...with steadfast and intentional determination, do the same with the Lord. Regardless of the obstacles, He will help you get through your natural/spiritual hurtles, with Christ's coaching...and an open heart!

Practice Is Over...Go Live!

Throughout your spiritual life you may have been preparing, training, memorizing, adjusting...getting to be an 'expert' in the Word...

Only that you've never actually applied it.

Now comes the time to bring the Word to life in your heart, reviving it!

Just remember that all meaningful communications with God must be active and intentional, coming from your heart, as if God is standing right in front of you...

Jesus spoke with God on a heartfelt and intentional level all the time, one-on-one.

You will now do the same; all it needs is execution...

Chapter 20

Best Spiritual Defense Is A Spiritual Offensive

You've heard the term "The best defense is a good offense" or other phrases worded similarly? Usually you hear such terms in sports, or other activities where a defensive posture is not to your advantage: instead, your best defense is to push forward and break whatever barrier is holding you back.

And that includes the spiritual: a Spiritual Offensive.

What is this "Spiritual Offensive"?

It's a renewed surge within you: a personal decision to intentionally push clear of the spiritual defensive that The Enemy has cleverly positioned to block your away toward God and Jesus.

Let's look at some key words that can define your spiritual offensive:

learning (not ignorant);
active (not lazy);
interested (not indifferent);
remembering (not forgetful);
pre-approved;

expecting;
revived;
reaching out intentionally;
trusting;
hoping;
loving...

Re-alignment From Defense To Offense

Satan loves to keep your faith on the defensive; instead of moving forward in your communcations with The Lord, The Enemy reduces your contact with God to a defensive position: always reaching out through fear, doubt, complaining, falling into rituals that make you feel good but have no contact with the spiritual.

Your challenges in life may have been pushing you backward in both your natural and spiritual progress; yet your hopeful spirit can't help wanting to break out of your defensive cover and to find yourself back and rekindled with God:

"My soul yearns for you in the night; my spirit within me earnestly seeks you (Isaiah 26:9, ESV)..."

It's in your God-given nature to express your emotions, your passions (you are born to communicate, remember?); suppressing them is unhealthy and unnatural to the human condition.

Just as you yearn to express your passion about something, channel some of it to express spiritually good and noble intentions that will re-align you to God...stay away from adding more Temptations, Distractions and Complications!

The Right Choices

Have you realized that every choice you've made so far has played a life-changing role in your life-journey? Every decision, every action, every emotion, deep or superficial, has determined the course of your life...?

The same holds true in your spiritual journey: choosing to launch a spiritual offensive will play a life-changing role in unifying your spiritual, natural, emotional, and supernatural life...

You will sense a new you:

"Therefore, if anyone is in Christ, he is a new creation; the old has passed away; behold, the new has come (2 Corinthians 5:17, ESV);"

Open your heart to a new attitude: the loving, intentional, spiritual advance as Jesus did...always looking steadfastly forward toward reconciliation with God:

"And let steadfastness have its full effect, that you may be perfect and complete, lacking in nothing (James 1:4, ESV)..."

Stay the course to your reunion-relationship with God, and give Him some room in your heart to draw close to you:

"Draw near to God, and he will draw near to you (James 4:8, ESV)..."

Start witnessing life-changing circumstances re-aligning in your favor:

"Every good gift and every perfect gift is from above, coming down from the Father of lights with whom there is no variation or shadow (James 1:17, ESV)..."

Appropriate blessings falling into place without your effort:

"And my God shall supply all your needs according to his riches in glory by Christ Jesus (Philippians 4:19, NKJV)..."

And to understand your importance as one who is pre-approved:

"...you are a chosen race, a royal priesthood, a holy nation, a people for his own possession, that you may proclaim the excellencies of him who called you out of darkness into his marvelous light (1 Peter 2:9, ESV)...

You are chosen, pre-approved. By intentionally opening your heart to God, you are inviting Him to help re-align your thinking and to feed your forward-advance; it starts with teaspoonfuls of blessings that you can handle...and afterward with tablespoons, glassfulls, bucket-sized, and ocean-sized blessings...!

You will no longer take a spiritually defensive posture by complaining, blaming, and "playing religion". Take your spiritual race to the next level; you are a hungry and passionate contender who is chasing the ultimate prize: reconciliation with God...

Show Him: demonstrate your confident trust in God by choosing to let go of the defensive posture in your spiritual life...take the inner offensive and let Him come into your heart, mind, soul and spirit...invite Him in.

As a pre-approved child of the most High God, release the emotion, the heartfelt passion that God gave you; use it to demonstrate your lovingkindness to both the world around you, and to Him.

Do what Jesus did: take a pro-active stance and reach out to the Father, the same way you reach out to someone you love (your husband, your wife, your children, your friends)...with heartfelt unifying intention!

Understand that God is the Architect of this universe; remain confident that He gave you the gift of communications so you live a balanced life in both the natural and spiritual world; to make the right choices, to always keep your heart open and welcome Him into your life with trusting love, and without fear:

"God gave us a spirit not of fear but of power and love and self-control (2 Timothy 1:7, ESV);"

"Therefore do not throw away your confidence, which has a great reward. For you have need of endurance, so that when you have done the will of God you may receive what is promised (Hebrews 10:35-36, ESV)."

God gave you the power, the understanding of what heartfelt desire can achieve; and as an athlete trained for endurance, you too can train your spirit and direct it toward the great reward...your spiritual reunification with God.

If you have understood this, then your entire mindset changes: a realization that you are not alone in this universe, not separated as The Enemy wants you to be. You are in the company of the spiritual realm in a physical world; knowing and understanding this will launch you into a spiritual offensive, knowing and expecting:

1. Vibrant understanding both your natural and spiritual self;
2. Renewal of your heartfelt intention of reaching out to God;
3. Confidence in the guidance of His Word in Christ;
4. Humble, fearless trust in Him as you build a spiritual momentum;
5. Feeling the 'nearness' to God, uniting with Him;
6. A spiritual revival similar to a Father-to-child relationship...

Your progress to reconciliation with God starts as soon as you have **DECIDED** to recondition your mindset to take affirmative action; Ignorance-Laziness-Indifference and Forgetfulness (Satan's Weapons of Total Chaos) cannot hold back your passion to push forward; just realizing that you are much more important to God than originally thought is enough to make you draw closer to Him...

You'll just want to go for it!

Action-Packed Life, Action-Packed Faith

Have you ever enjoyed doing something? Enjoying a game of golf, love working at your job, going on vacation, sitting down to eat, workout at the gym, listening to music, arranging your garden, painting a portrait, playing with your kids, etc...there are thousands of interesting activities that spark your decision to take action. You set your mind on something because you are interested in **doing something you like and benefit from.**

The same thing occurs when you decide to revive your reunification to God: you **become interested** in reaching out to the spiritual because you are interested in **doing something you like to benefit from!** At the same time, keep in mind that Satan is trying to prevent any re-unification!

So go ahead and pursue (for example) your career, caring for your kids, loving your spouse, enjoying sports, meeting your challenges head-on, cooking that barbeque steak...etc; live your life with a balanced sense of goodness and with renewed intention...

Now do the same with your relationship with God: extend the same passion and reach out to revive your personal relationship with The Lord, knowing that better days are coming with God in your daily life! Upgrade your newly discovered-but-poorly-used gift of communication and bring it up to a higher standard; and use the eye-opening knowledge of the secret evils coming from Ignorance-Laziness-Indifference and Forgetfulness against you to keep you focused, alert.

You also have a trusted companion to assist you:

"The Lord is my strength and my shield; in him my heart trusts, and I am helped; my heart exults, and with my song I give thanks to him (Psalm 28:7, ESV)."

A Power To Be Respected

Imagine you had the power to launch a nuclear missile; imagine the enormous power you have under control, and imagine the great responsibility that came with such ability!

A spiritual offensive is a powerful, emotional, inner expression of faith; it is God-inspired, and is a personal tool to be used solely for re-unification with Him. Misusing it for other purposes can turn against you or not work at all! Remember to "not take the name of the Lord your God in vain (Exodus 20:7, ESV)."

152

Yet even here, at the closest proximity you've ever been to God, you will find Satan's Weapons Of Total Chaos trying to sabotage your well-intentioned actions: Temptations-Distractions and Complications in your life are fertile ground for The Enemy to divert your passion away from a joyous relationship with the Lord. They can distort your God-given power as you can be tempted to become selfish, judgemental, suppressive...

Problem: With The Enemy engaging in his own offensive against you, how can you possibly avoid being distracted from God's blessings in your life?

Answer: re-set your mind to seek the **"things above (Col. 2)."**

How do you that?

A passionate "go and get it" attitude has something to do with it.

Go and Get It

Do you have an overriding interest for something, or even someone?

For example: interest in pursuing your career, caring for your kids, completing your college course, loving your spouse, buying your new car, listening to music, collect sports memorabillia, etc..?

What do you do?

You **GO AND GET IT !**

You would engage your heart and soul (and some good sense) to get it, pushing aside any distraction that comes against you...right?

It is the same thing in the spiritual; you must have an equally **overriding interest** for reconciliation with God, pushing aside any evil distractions The Enemy places in front of you!

You see, spiritual goals require the same emotional attraction that you would ordinarily have for earthly ones: you want it because you are interested in it...and ignoring distractions.

In this case, your overriding interest is not just reconciling with God; you also acknowledge that you understand that Satan is attempting to sabotage and separate you from any relationship with the Lord by any means possible...

You've become aware, awakened...

Simply knowing this changes your spiritual direction: it can clear your mind from any obstacle that may obstruct your journey to God.

And you are not left alone: The Lord supplies His Word that contains the **easiest, most gentle** instructions you can ever use; just open your mind and heart to Him so that He senses your yearning to learn and understand.

Here is one instruction given by Jesus to a tired and yearning heart:

"Come to me , all you who are weary and burdened and I will give you rest. Take my yoke upon you and learn from me, for I am gentle and humble in heart, and you will find rest for your souls. For my yoke is easy and my burden is light (Matthew 11:28-30, NIV)."

Show Your Heartfelt Gratitude...Don't Suppress it

Do you remember moments in your life when someone did you a kindness?

Example: someone bought you coffee at the office (you had forgotten your wallet at home); a friend helped you with a personal problem; a co-worker assisted you with a difficult task; a stranger helped you change your flat tire; you fell down and someone helped you stand up...etc?

Didn't you feel grateful for the kindness you received?

Gratitude (or thankfulness) opens up your heart to a natural, humble goodness. It communicates inner relief, spiritual peace.

And it shows when you are at peace!

So why not show the same gratitude to God for any kindness received:

"So, whether you eat or drink, or whatever you do, do all to the glory of God (1 Corinthians 10:31, ESV)."

Open your grateful heart, your soul, and your reaching to God. It is an intentional act that expresses thankfulness for the reconciliation received, just as you are thankful to those you love.

Just reach out to Him in gratitude...see how love overwhelms you!

It's All About Position...Of Your Heart

Too often you place your heart in a defensive position because you are unprepared spiritually, and Satan can take advantage of it to cause separation; he can easily pull you in any direction.

And it's so easy to do these days: bombarded with materialism, advertising, selfish want, 'me first,' etc...so many distractions!

This is where Ignorance, Laziness, Indifference, and Forgetfulness come to interfere with your natural life, ending up abandoning spiritual goals, and forever keeping yourself cut-off from God.

As mentioned in the Introduction, you've likely been positioning your focus on what you thought were "the reasons" behind all your earthly and spiritual lack; you've been decoyed and left running around in circles, chasing after the RESULTS of your disconnection, while the ACTUAL CAUSES are cleverly concealed and continue their secret offensive in your spiritual and earthly life (take a moment and re-read the Introduction)...

That's taking the defensive...

But now, all of The Enemy's battle plans have been exposed; you can re-group your spiritual passion for a new offensive against the actual source of your spiritual disconnection!

Chapter 21

Taking The Heartfelt Offensive

"...with You I can run up against a troop...(Psalm 18:29)."

Is your motivation built up at this point? Are you ready to run up against the 'enemy troops' (in other words the natural and spiritual challenges) in your life with the Lord as your back-up?

Of course you are ready...you've had plenty of experience going on the offensive (some examples):

-Studied hard to graduate through college;
-Made mistakes in life, but picked yourself up and kept going;
-Helped some friends in need;
-Defended situations you thought were right;
-Gave advice to people who needed it;
-Showed yourself a good and valued employee;
-Controlled your finances;
-Went to rehab;
-Nurtured a special relationship with a person you care for;
-Slowly paid off your credit card debt;
-Got married;
-Painted the kitchen;

-Quit your job for another one;
-Texted a friend;
-Walked to the convenience store...etc.

Almost every daily action you've taken, thousands of them, are based on a PERSONAL DECISION to be pro-active, to take the offensive...

Even reading this book is a decision to take action!

It's no different with God. Once you decide to interact with Him, your mind and spirit voluntarily (and intentionally) reach out in supernatural reconciliation...

Get That Feeling...By Thinking And Speaking

Have you ever felt that feeling, a heartfelt desire to be near someone:

Your husband/wife;
Your children;
A close friend;
Your sister;
Your brother;
A co-worker;
Your pastor;
Your boss;
Your country...etc?

You know the feeling: it is desire for belonging, togetherness; it is a gentle and intentional closeness that makes you feel at ease, relieved, caring, safe...

158

So what do you do?

You communicate good and noble intentions to those important to you: your spouse, your kids, your friends, your pets, your co-workers...

The spoken words that come out of your mouth is a result of your mind wanting to express something loving, caring to those you love and respect.

This is what communication is all about: aligning your knowledge, thinking...and then expressing it outwards with words...

Hopefully they will be words of lovingkindness...

Being close to God is no different: you desire an intense spiritual closeness to Him that makes you feel at ease, relieved, and safe.

It helps to understand that you are already pre-approved to draw near God: He was the One who has given you the incredible ability to communicate...you've been **pre-approved** and equipped to get closer with the Father; through the power of Love as Jesus showed, you can now shift forward with honorable intention toward reconciliation...

Speak It

In Chapter 17, it was mentioned that you need to personalize your communications with God, to simply talk with Him about your confidence you have in His ability to steer your life physically and spiritually...

To help you start in your journey of spiritual interaction with God, use the Bible and its verses to gently ease you into communications with God.

For example, take a look at some verses from the Book of Psalms Chapter 18 (using the New King James Version), and read it out loud:

I will love You,O Lord, my strength.
The Lord is my rock and my fortress and my deliverer;
My God, my strength, in whom I trust;
My shield and the horn of my salvation, my stronghold.
I will call upon the Lord, *who is worthy* to be praised; So shall I be saved from my enemies (Ps 18:1-3)...

Here's another:

You have also given me the shield of your salvation;
Your right hand has held me up,
Your gentleness has made me great.
You enlarged my path under me,
So my feet did not slip (Ps 18:35-36)...

Notice the encouraging words such as: my strength, my rock, my fortress, my deliverer, my salvation, my stronghold, etc...these are power words; they are meant to re-align your inner self, your mentality, your psychology...your communications...toward a loving and spiritually intimate contact with God. Remember that your communications must be loving and heartfelt...as those you genuinely love here on earth.

160

You will eventually evolve to the point where you too will express heartfelt words on your own to God...with the Bible always helping you to re-focus; it is an indispensable tool.

Just as you would say to your spouse (example): "sweetheart, I can't do this on my own, and I would really appreciate it if you can help me..." or, to your son to help you with a task (example)...

You get the point: you need to reach out with heartfelt interest in order to make a connection with anyone in this world.

God is no different: project your communications to Him honorably and intentionally...lovingly!

Remember in Chapter 9 (God Is Not) that God is not just some kind of 'complaint department or genie in a bottle that waits on your command...' so don't treat Him that way!

Watchful

Being watchful (some may even call it PAYING ATTENTION, or BEING CAREFUL) is an active, forward-thinking, intentional act of communication: you are checking, concentrating, surveying, paying attention, testing, measuring circumstances to see how they are going to affect your life.

You already have experience being watchful in your life:

-watchful of your family's well-being and security;
-watchful of your performance at work;
-paying attention to your finances;

-controlling your golf shot;
-your health;
-when driving your car;
-of your relationships;
-watchful when you cross the street;
-performance of your investments;
-cooking on the stove...etc.

Even Jesus teaches you to remain watchful:

"Watch out that you are not deceived (Luke 21:8, NIV)," and:

"Be always on the watch...(Luke 21:36)..."

Watchfulness is an intentional, heartfelt act; just as you are watchful
of the things you love in your natural life, extend your watchfulness
(or pay attention, or be careful) to the spiritual:

-your heartfelt re-unification with God;
-of devious circumstances aimed to disconnect you;
-falling into Ignorance-Laziness-Indifference-Forgetfulness;
-not be Tempted and Distracted into bad Complications;
-of neglecting The Word in Jesus as your gentle guide;
-using the Word in your life;
-that your intentions are truly good and noble;
-grateful for the supernatural blessings in your life;
-understanding what Jesus' coaching is really doing for you...

Be intentionally watchful in the spiritual, as you do with your life
(examples: you brush your hair to look nice, adjust your tie to look
presentable, wash your car so that it is sparkling clean, cut the grass
and trim the hedges to look nice, enjoying a special moment, etc.).

A Great Opportunity

When an opportunity invites you to:

1. Welcome the Love of God in your life;
2. Revitalize your life in both the natural and spiritual;
3. Expect unexpected gifts of blessings and favor;
4. Feel a Love within you that has no boundaries...

You know what happens: You'll want to know more of God (not Ignorant); with motivation (and not Lazy); interested to reach out to Him (and not Indifferent); absorb the growing knowledge in your mind (and not Forget). Your interest becomes passionate, your intentions, heartfelt...

Your opportunity has come to join and remain in God's Winners' Circle!

Abandon your position of 'defensive religion' and go on the heartfelt inner offensive with all the love in you in expectation for re-unification with the Lord!

You already have the right tool: your gift of communications!

But now you may have a problem...actually it's a good problem: You may feel that you've wasted a great deal of time away from The Lord; an urgency may be surfacing in you: you can't afford to be Lazy any more, YOU'VE GOT TO GET YOURSELF GOING!

And like anything new in your life, you need instructions to start your new journey...this is where your heartfelt offensive requires guidance, to give you proper direction.

A Father-To-Child Relationship

In Christ, you find some of the most gentle words ever written to launch you forward in the spiritual: they can bring out the passionate lovingkindness in you. He prepares you to interact with God in a Father-To-Child relationship.

With Jesus' gentle message, you become uncontainable; you just want to go for it! Nothing can hold you back: you've been pre-approved for eternal salvation, covered in a spiritual blanket of love and peace:

"Very truly I tell you , whoever hears my word and believes him who sent me has eternal life and will not be judged but has crossed over from death to life (John 5:24, NIV)..."

There is no need to be intimidated from life's challenges any more: believe that Christ has brought your salvation; as a father, God will supply supernatural support, and help strengthen you to take the heartfelt offensive to deal with any circumstances in your life with proper conduct...even when the tragedies come:

"And my God will supply every need of yours according to his riches in glory in Christ Jesus (Philippians 4:9, ESV)."

Grab the opportunity:

a) re-align your mind. Think about God and His free gift to you: your power to communicate with Him;

164

b) understand who you are to God: pre-approved to communicate.
c) watch how The Enemy is infiltrating your soul;
d) open your loving heart and welcome God in your life...
e) make His Word your weapon of choice, with Jesus your coach;
f) trust that the Lord is working on your behalf...

Look at the first word of each point above:

're-align,'
'understand,'
'watch,'
'open,'
'make,'
'trust...'

These are action words. Everything that you do in life is action; and every action must be examined to see if it is good and noble before you continue, because The Enemy is always on the lookout to sabotage any action that leads you to your walk with Jesus...

That's why you must always be watchful and determine if your spiritual offensive has God's blessings or not:

"Dear friends, do not believe every spirit, but test the spirits to see whether they are from God, because many FALSE PROPHETS have gone out into the world (1 John 4:1)."

Being watchful makes it harder for The Enemy to:

-compromise your gift of communications;
-deceive you with Ignorance-Laziness-Indifference-Forgetfulness;
-trap you into Temptations that Distract and Complicate;

-sabotage your relationship with God;
-lose your freedom in Christ;
-lose your joy;
-make you think God isn't interested in you;
-ignore God;
-anger you due to your life's shortcomings;
-ignite conflicting emotions in you;
-frustrate you;
-make you feel 'un-approved;'
-suppress your heartfelt desire to stay in contact with God;
-interfere in your daily life;
-defeat you psychologically;
-lay blame at God for your troubles...etc.

"Being watchful is too complicated," you might say...but is it?

Take lessons from your life. Consider this (examples):

"Are you careful when crossing the street?"
"Are you watchful that the baby doesn't fall out of its crib?"
"Are you mindful not to touch a hot stove...etc?

Being watchful in the spiritual is no different; it should be natural to you: just extend your watchfulness in the spiritual as well!

Even if you do stumble and fall from some kind of circumstance in your life, reach out to God who is waiting for you to look at Him with your heart so that:

"...out of His glorious riches He may strengthen you with power through His Spirit in your inner being (Ephesians 3:16, NIV)..."

It may not be easy at first; it is normal that doubt and frustration can set in...and that's what The Enemy wants from you: frustration, discouragement, and a whole list of emotions that are meant to cut off any of your intentional efforts to re-unite with God, even before you start...but:

You must take the inner offensive and decide you want to change your mindset; that you want to be in contact with The Lord. Do not be discouraged by overwhelming circumstances in your life; take a moment, just look up to God with renewed vigor and heartfelt faith:

"...one thing I do: forgetting what lies behind and straining forward to what lies ahead, I press toward the goal for the prize of the upward call of God in Christ Jesus (Philippians 3:13-14, ESV)..."

Take Heartfelt Action

Look at your life: with all your challenges in life, do you still love (for example) your spouse, your child, your best friend, your mother (or father, sister, brother), your country, etc?

Everyone has some kind of deep passion for someone or something, regardless of what challenges they face...can you associate the same deep passion for God the same way?

Can you say to yourself (example): "As I love my family dearly and I want them to show that I care for their safety and their love, I want you Lord to sense my love for you...?"

Jesus understood how powerful communication can be in any relationship...it touches peoples' hearts either in a good or bad way;

he showed that Love is the preferred expression of communication that brings people together. Are you willing to take on the heartfelt offensive and communicate the same loving expressions of communication to God as you would with someone you care for?

Invite God to sense your heartfelt longing for His fellowship, longing to join His Winners' Circle. Use the same longing you normally use in daily life and reach out to Him!

SHOW Him that you care, longing for Him to sense your desire for a spiritual relationship (just as you show your genuine love and trust to your wife/husband, kids, friends...right?).

So walk on top of those 'mountains': the mountains of fear, of uncertainty, of your debts, of your lost opportunities, of your troubled marriage, of your ill-health, of your envy of others, of your jealousy, your anger...etc, and take heartfelt action: look to the Lord with loving trust to overcome your challenges EVERY DAY!

All this may seem difficult to do and believe (old bad habits are hard to break, including the doubt that God can change your circumstances); but it's up to you to re-align your mind, to pay attention, to be watchful, to communicate, to take re-unifying action by opening your heart to trusting God. The Word shows you how do it, because God is:

"...my refuge, a strong tower against the foe...(Ps.. 61:3, NIV)"

God has always been there; it's up to you to reach out and bring your life to a critical shift...towards Him...

168

Chapter 22

The Critical Shifts

From this day forward, your life will undergo critical shifts: you will begin to think differently about who you are; the REAL importance of your good and noble deeds, and the meaning of your life both in the natural and spiritual dimension...you are more important than you think!

Your life isn't irrelevant...it isn't just to pay bills, work, and worry...

On the contrary, you are **EXTREMELY IMPORTANT** to God's plan!

And this is why The Enemy is so dedicated in rendering you spiritually paralyzed, falling victim to Satan's Weapons Of Total Chaos: he already knows how important you are...and wants to keep that awareness away from your knowing it!

There is no greater moment in history, where your powers of communication are so important, so critical...it is a period where your clear mindset is required: watchful, attentive...

Do you remember that in Chapter 1 you found out you were born for communication, verbally, physically, mentally, **and** spiritually?

Think about it: from the moment you wake up, to going back to bed in the evening, you are communicating with everything that surrounds you in a verbal, physical, mental, and even mystical manner!

Can you map out how you communicate every day?

Here's a little help from a simple example:

-you wake up, still in bed;
-you body-stretch;
-possibly start thinking about the day ahead;
-you decide to get yourself out of bed: bathroom, etc;
-the dog needs to be fed and walked;
-pour yourself a cup of coffee;
-turn on the tv to get the latest weather report, the news, etc.
-your wife/husband also gets up...start the chit-chat;
-you wake up the kids for breakfast before going to school, etc...

You get the point: from the moment you are awake and conscious, you begin interacting with your world...you are communicating with it (the moment you reach out to turn off the alarm clock in the morning, you are reaching out in communication; by starting to think in bed about the day ahead, you are interacting, communicating; by pouring yourself a cup of coffee, you are communicating...face it: you are communication!).

Anything that you do is communication...even by placing that empty cup of coffee in the sink is an interaction created by you...

There are some communications however that are more critical than others.

For instance, have you ever experienced a moment when you wanted to confide in someone that you can trust?

Take your best friend for example: he/she has always been a person you could open up to, talk about anything, emptying out your heart. Don't you feel safe and secure confiding in your friend, a person who understands you? It's an inner desire to reveal what's on your mind to someone close to you, at every level of communicating: verbally (words), physically (gestures, physical posture), mentally (expressing thoughts), psychologically (your attitude), spiritually: your inner joys, your problems...

This inner desire to come out and communicate is isn't just limited to the natural: your inner self desires to take it further...

Critical Shift #1: your natural life is only the beginning

Your interaction with the natural world is only a starting point; as you grow and mature, you will sense that your natural ability to communicate is only a stepping stone toward the spiritual realm.

You've already felt the need for spiritual contact: Example, have you ever wondered why your mind is sometimes attracted to the vast expanse of the night sky with all its stars? Or the serene peace and quiet of a lovely stroll in the forest? Or sitting quietly by a crackling fire? Or gazing out at the immense ocean as you sit by the beach...? Or the creative fairytale stories about mystical powers...?

In quiet moments of serene peace, your mind reaches out to the immense majesty of this world, thinking and wondering..."

It's not only because "you want to relax" or "you like fantasies..."

It isn't only about inner quiet or "Zen time."

It's about receiving a mysterious feeling of reaching out to another avenue of communication-interaction on a different dimension, a spiritual one.

Your inner self needs it, demands it, and seeks out to find it...

Face it: this universe is about communication at every level, at every dimension...and understanding this starts here, now, in the natural world, your world, your life!

It starts with everything that you've read in the previous chapters:

1) understanding your own self, who you really are (Ch.1);
2) the obstacles that contaminate your inner nature (Ch. 2,3,4);
3) the Enemy who is behind your distortion and deprivation;
4) your exciting comeback...

Your natural life is only the beginning of something wonderful!

Critical Shift #2: detect the clues in your life

Your entire natural life provides the clues as to how to conduct yourself to the spiritual; everything that you do, think, feel, can be associated with the spiritual. For example:

a) you did honest and genuine good deeds;
b) you accomplished something that made you happy;
c) made some mistakes in life and are making a good comeback;
d) you love and respect the people around you...etc.

You normally do good deeds in order to be considered worthy by others, and face it, it makes you feel good!

Do you realize that you can also offer all the good and noble things that you do here on earth as an offering to God?

Just as you want to prove your worthiness to someone here on earth, show the same worthiness to The Creator; take the step, and **intentionally** show your good intentions here on earth, and to Him!

Example: do you want to do the best that you can for your wife, your husband, your brother/sister, friends, colleagues? Have you decided to give the best of yourself at home, at work, with your friends, your family?

Do the same with God! Confide with God lovingly, open up to Him, and show Him that whatever you do here on earth that is noble and good is a reflection of what you'd like to do with God: share your life with him, your tasks, your feelings:

"God did this so that they would seek him and perhaps reach out for him and find him, though he is not far from any of us. For in him we live and move and have our being (Acts 17:27,28, NIV)."

By understanding this incredible wisdom, you will sense within yourself a growing feeling of wanting a togetherness with Him; to share every moment of your waking life with Him.

So this is the second critical shift: share the emotion of your heartfelt kindness and your intentionally good deeds here on earth

173

with the The Lord who gave you the ability to do so. Reach out with the same intentions at the spiritual level: seek out "the things above (Colossians 3:2 NIV)..."

And when you do reach out, speak it with your mind, your heart, and your mouth; and it doesn't have to be complicated (examples):

"As I take my shower this morning Lord, let me thank you for letting me enjoy the water on my body, the water that you created for our benefit; and as I wash my body, wash me and cleanse away my mind, and my soul. Keep me clean and healthy in both mind, body, and spirit as I lovingly gaze upon you..."

"See Lord: I want to do things as complete as possible here on earth to please others and to please you Father..."

"As I am being genuinely polite and respectful to all Lord, I want to be the same with you dearest Lord..."

"All that I do, all that I think, all that I feel, I want to live it together with you my loving Father, together...forever..."

Critical Shift #3: Already Pre-approved And Equipped

You already have an advantage: you've been pre-approved and equipped with superior communications abilities to improve your current state of mind-body-soul-spirit (the same as if you were pre-approved for a credit-card, pre-approved for a promotion, pre-approved for a home loan...etc), and your contact with God.

It must come as a surprise to you that God has pre-approved and equipped you for contact with Himself,...

174

But you shouldn't be...

You've been pre-approved and equipped from the moment that you were conceived!

After all, what good is your communications ability if not to reach higher?

As you take care of your body, your hygiene, your hair, your teeth, etc...make the same loving effort with your gift of communications; Shift your mind to handle your gift of communication with greater respect, as something very precious; as in all things that are precious to you, you will be motivated to improve your personal interactions with your community, your family, your friends, even with yourself. It will naturally lead you to share the same good and noble interactions with God...

You no longer want to wrestle uselessly with Ignorance-Laziness-Indifference-Forgetfulness: you've been pre-approved so get out of that jam!

Remember this: **You are no longer a victim of Satan's Weapons of Total Chaos**; you are a pre-approved winner, freed and saved in Christ who helps you clear the communications-clutter in your life with heartfelt Love, without rituals and 'hocus-pocus...'

It merits a reminder of what Jesus said:

"Very truly I tell you , whoever hears my word and believes him who sent me has eternal life and will not be judged but has crossed over from death to life (John 5:24, NIV)..."

Once you sense in your heart that you've been physically and spiritually pre-approved all along, wouldn't you get a bit angry in yourself for having let this slip past you? It's the same way with Ignorance, Laziness, Indifference and Forgetfulness: you didn't understand their importance to your disconnection, until now!

And as you eagerly want to accomplish something important in your life, use the same eagerness to complete your life by 'cleaning up your inner house' (which is your heart, mind, soul, and spirit); re-align and claim the ultimate accomplishment: your pre-approved, clear communications channel with God. Your contact with Him becomes intentional, heartfelt...loving.

Critical Shift #4: In God's House

All this interaction brings a spiritually 'warm and fuzzy' feeling of belonging, sheltered in God's dwelling:

"...Lord, you have been our dwelling place (Ps 90:1, NIV);"

"...make the Most High your dwelling –even the Lord, who is my refuge (Ps 91:9, NIV);"

"...defender of widows, is God in His holy dwelling (Ps. 68:5, NIV);"

"...in your dwelling you keep them safe from accusing tongues (Ps.31:20, NIV)..."

A dwelling (or house) is a place of rest, of security, letting go of the burdens you faced in the day, sheltering you from the weather; it's no different in God's House: enter into God's House and let go of the burdens of the day to Him. Appreciate His restful embrace in

176

your heart as He shelters you from your storms...Satan's Weapons of Total Chaos will no longer hinder you; they remain outside God's House while you are sheltered inside, confident of His protection. As in any shelter, accept His gentle hospitality into your heart with gratitude; remain confident that He will feed you the restfulness of His wisdom that will re-align your life to receive your deserved, pre-approved blessings...!

Will your life change dramatically? Sometimes yes, and sometimes gradually as you learn and evolve in your physical and spiritual life. It is up to you to understand that God has a protective shelter for you, and to trust Him to change your circumstances for the better.

Critical Shift #5: Trusting God

How do you let yourself trust God?

Put it this way: how do you let yourself trust the people you are close to: your husband/wife, your best friend, your pastor, priest, spiritual guide...etc? You trust with your loving heart, expecting good things will come from them...and grateful for it.

It is no different with God: Trust that He and His Word will bless your good deeds...and don't forget to be thankful and grateful for what you received (and what you are going to receive)!

Jesus demonstrated his trust to God. Here's one simple example:

"And Jesus lifted up his eyes and said "Father, I thank you that you have heard me (John 11:41, ESV)."

God does hear you, and will respond to your genuine and heartfelt communications. How does He do it? Jesus describes it best in the parable of the Prodigal Son in Luke 15:11-32 ...

(If you haven't read the Parable of the Prodigal Son, read it and you will see how God considers you in His world: it's about a wayward son who squandered his indepenence and his inheritance; after he lost it all, and in remorse, he reached out to his father in trusting mercy to let him come back home...the father showed his wayward son mercy and restoration, because the FATHER LOVED HIS SON).

God will do the same for you: He will open His arms and unconditionally welcome you back home...

You can't help but thank God for His trusting mercy.

You already know the feeling of gratitude from your own life:

-How did you feel when someone thanked you for some good
 deed you did?
-Or, YOU gave thanks for one's kindness towards you?
-Grateful when you received a promotion?
-Thankful for being given free tickets to a sports event?
-Someone helped you change your flat tire on your car...etc?

It's called gratitude, a trusting thankfulness that is both humble and deeply personal: your thankfulness and behaviour communicates that you believe and acknowledge that someone has provided you a kindness...

If you can trust someone in this natural, imperfect world to do a kindness to you, then you can do the same with God who is perfect. Confide to God openly, communicate your desire to return to Him and the warm security of His House.

Tell God that you trust Him; use the experience in your life to formulate a similar statement of faith. Example:

"Lord, I know that The Enemy wants me out of contact with you, and is throwing all kinds of temptations and distractions at me...but I know I can find security in Your House...

I want to live my life with you in it, together Father. I know you are waiting for me to reach out to you, so here I am reaching out sincerely, honestly. I know I have done plenty of mistakes in my life, even intentionally distancing myself away from you. Sorry about that. I want to come back into your awesome presence, in communication with you as I am here on earth with others...

Let's be together forever Lord as I do the right and noble thing on earth with my family, my work, my leisure; only let's be together my dearest Lord..."

Release all your concerns, your insecurities, your fears to Him and concentrate on your new-found love relationship with God; simply express your admiration and confidence in His ability to turn your life around, the same kind of trust as with someone you trust here on earth...

Are you drawn to persons who show they can be trusted? It's no different with God: draw toward Him with unwavering trust that He does consider your good and thankful heart...

179

It will come to you when you trust His Word, but most importantly, it will come when you have genuine trust in Him!

Consider this: Just as you naturally expect that "day eventually turns into night," trust that God will mysteriously intervene in your life; it's that real. You will start to sense goodness embracing you as you humbly reach out to Him. It is implanted within you: *know and trust* that God is working to align good things in your life:

Fixing your marriage or starting a new life;
Stopping your drug-addiction;
Reducing your debts;
Controlling your anger;
Stopping your hate;
Building up your confidence;
Doing greater good works;
Progress in a business venture;
Bring inner peace to your spirit;
Helping others;
Relying less on 'religion' and trusting God Himself...etc.

Trust requires the same inner energy as faith: it requires VOLUNTARY ACTION WITHIN YOURSELF to activate your trust (remember chapter 20:"The Best Spiritual Defense Is A Spiritual Offensive?").... Remember what the Bible states about faith without works (in other words, without action):

"What does it profit, my brethren, if someone says he has faith but does not have works? Can faith save him? If a brother or sister is naked and destitute of daily food, and one of you says to them, "Depart in peace, be warmed and filled," but you do not give them the things which are needed for the body, what does it profit? Thus also faith by itself, if it does not have works, *is dead* (James 2:14-17, NKLV)."

Logical isn't it? Faith without any action (or works) is dead...

It is the same as saying:

-if you don't work, you don't get paid;
-if you don't change your attitude, then you won't improve;
-if you won't water the plant, it will not grow...etc.

The message is clear: **you've got to take action to get a result.**

Trust is the same: it is action, based on the belief that you can count on someone to do the right and honorable thing (or someone trusts that YOU will do the right and honorable thing for them)...

Trust is an important, intentional act of communication!

So do the same with God: reach out to God...with genuine trust!

Critical Shift #6: Activate Faith...With Your Natural Life (expanding on Critical Shift #2)

In Critical Shift #2, it was mentioned that your life is full of clues as to how to re-align yourself to God: by showing your good-will intentions to both people AND to God.

Sometimes however, the love in your heart needs a small

boost to keep it invigorated and alive...

You see, life and its challenges will always creep in at moments where you are not paying attention, and steal the connected relationship that you have in the Spirit...regardless of your depth in faith...

So aside from understanding that your natural life is only the beginning of your journey (Critical Shift 1), your ability to detect the clues you need for connection (Critical Shift 2), your pre-approval (Critical Shift 3), staying in God's House (Critical Shift 4), and Trusting God (Critical Shift 5)...you will also need (believe it or not) help from the natural world!

(*** This is a very important shift in your faith-filled life)

Sometimes, you must boost your faith in God by speaking about good things that worked for you in the natural world, associating these with your inner communications to God.

Examples:

"Lord, just as I say 'good morning' to my darling husband/wife, I say hello to you this morning..."

"Just as tend to my rose garden by watering it, pruning, and lovingly arranging it...I equally tend to my faith in you my God as Jesus so lovingly showed me..."

"As I take the inititative to clean my house and keep it from getting messy...I do the same with my heart and soul by preventing them from falling into the mess of Ignorance, Laziness, Indifference, and Forgetfulness..."

182

"Father, as I thank my co-workers for a job well done, I want to thank you for giving me the power to reach out and communicate with heartfelt intention to you..."

"As I love my children dearly and care for my relationship with them, I reach out to you with the same care Father so I can be together with you all the days of my life..."

"As my wife/husband go through the pleasures and challenges of life together, I invite you Lord to walk with us together, be part of us, let your lovingkindness fill our hearts with the joy of complete trust in you..."

"Lord, you were always in my heart, but I never realized it. But now I do understand that you've been there all the while...I only needed to adjust my signal out to you. You've been waiting for me all along Lord, and now I desire to live the rest of my life together with you..."

These were a few examples on how you can get yourself closer to God by using the good and noble intentions of earthly life, and apply these feelings to the reach out in the spiritual!

Just as you *decide* to speak to be heard...
Just as you *wave* your hand to say hello from a distance...
Just as you *reach down* to pick up someone who fell down...
Just as you *smile* when you see someone you know...
Just as you *push* a button to start a car...
Just as you *turn* the doorknob to open a door...
Just as you *say* the words 'I love you' to acknowledge your feelings to someone special...etc.

You get the picture: any good and noble decisions, any actions you do on earth can be used to reach out to the Lord.

Let's say you have a problem with worrying too much...what would be the action you must take?

First of all, worry (or any other negative situation) not only makes your life miserable; it is also a way for The Enemy to cut you off from communications with The Lord.

Now, you know better: as pre-approved to communicate on a spiritual level, and knowing how Satan's Weapons Of Total Chaos disconnect you from God, you can take the Spiritual Offensive and speak out to any circumstance with authority:

"Father God, you know that I am worried and I can't help feeling that way; I know that The Enemy is attacking me with worry so he can cut me off from you. But I can never betray the ones that I love...so as I love my wife, my friends, and never betray them, I am always devoted to you my Father and will never betray or abandon our union together. You leave me with peace, you give me peace, and you do not to let my heart be troubled and not to be afraid (referring to John 14:27), so I will open my heart in trust and will set aside my worry as I gaze at your marvelous glory..."

(this is just an example; use as many or a few words that are comfortable to you, but conveying the same meaning as above)

And what does the Lord do?

He will sense your eager anticipation for divine relations; and you know what? He will shift your circumstances to help you find your peace in any situation, or strengthen you to overcome the worry...you just keep your spiritual love-relationship with God alive and vibrant as you do with those you love...!

God can help in so many unexpected ways...that's why it is best to re-align your heart-mind-soul and spirit in expectation of unexpected blessings and favour (Chapter 17) while you lovingly maintain your personal relationship with Him.

Don't expect Him to buy you a yacht or make you a millionaire...such expectations are purely selfish and self-serving. God knows what you need, so don't lose your focus: God isn't a genie to control on your command...He will give you what you need, and maybe a little more if He feels it will not destroy your faith in Him...

Critical Shift #7: Natural And Spiritual In Harmony

Some wrongly believe that spirituality means to either disconnect from the natural and enter into the realm of the spiritual through some kind of "spiritual trance"; or perform repetitive, symbolic religious rituals over and over again...oftentimes the ritual becomes more important than your faith...no spirituality in them other than a 'feel-good' state of mind...

Separating the natural from the spiritual will not work; the natural and spiritual must complement each other so that you can become an effective communicator with God:

"Now may the God of peace himself sanctify you completely, and may your <u>whole spirit and soul and body</u> be kept

blameless at the coming of the our Lord Jesus Christ (1 Thessalonians 5:23, ESV)..."

"Be kind to one another, tenderhearted, forgiving one another, as God in Christ forgave you (Ephesians 4:32 ESV)..."

"But the Fruit of the Spirit is love, joy, peace, forebearance, kindness, goodness, faithfulness, gentleness and self-control...(Galatians 5:22-23 NIV)..."

"A new commandment I give to you, that you love one another: just as I have loved you, you also are to love one another (John 13:34 ESV)..."

"Little children, let us not love in word or talk but in deed and in truth (1John 3:18 ESV)..."

"Love must be sincere. Hate what is evil; cling to what is good (Romans 12:9)..."

As you can see, the verses above convey instructions for both your natural and spiritual...not just for the spiritual alone; besides, all good thoughts, words, and deeds in your life begin in your inner self, but are demonstrated in your natural life. You must exercise your inner intention to gather your mind-soul-spirit and body to seek God's attention. Your spirit cannot be spiritual on its own...

And check this out:

"you've already experienced something like that..."

186

Surprised?

Here's the proof (for example):

"Have you ever felt a sense of total contentment inside and out from some wonderful experience: falling in love; paying off your mortgage; doing well on the job; on a two-week vacation on a tropical island; relaxing at home with a good book; enjoying supper at your favorite restaurant...?

You get the point: the feeling is one of inner and outer satisfaction which is connected to an experience in your life...

But this balance of your natural and spiritual self does not stop there: your natural and spiritual self needs to go further and find the natural and spiritual contentment with God.

Remember that you've been implanted with the power to communicate on BOTH the natural and spiritual level...so:

"Can you achieve the same feeling with God, a natural-spiritual connection balance?"

You now realize that yes, you can!

Now you might say, "well I believe in God, but I'm still in debt...my wife hates me...my car is old and I can't afford another one...my kid needs braces...gotta' pay daughter's college tuition...I feel depressed that I can't see progress in my life...I don't know why I'm alive...no one loves me...I feel alone...I'm losing my hair...I'm not as good-looking as I was...I'm afraid...I'm uncertain about my future...etc."

True, balancing the natural and spiritual while you wrestle with your necessities may not seem easy, and not all issues will be resolved overnight...but they are not impossible to overcome!

Don't lose sight that your primary role is communication...you were born with it, implanted by God in you so that you can ultimately reach a lovely balance in the natural and spiritual...

Don't let Ignorance, Laziness, Indifference, and Forgetfulness prevent you from gaining this incredible balance...

God's intervention happens to followers of Christ, but your mind is the trigger that releases God's power in the body-soul-spirit: it takes a **re-alignment of your thinking** to balance your natural with your spiritual.

Whatever you say and do is a physical result of what's in your mind, your thinking. **You decide** whether to think and do positive things in your life and use the same feelings and intentions to reach out to God; or remain a victim of Satan's Weapons of Total Chaos and repeat the same negative thoughts-words-and-deeds that have kept you down...so why not shift toward the positive choice and become free in God's Winners' Circle...?

Critical Shift #8: Use The Word...And Free Yourself

Use the Word, the easy-read instructions of Christ; The Word releases you to communicate with God in a close and personal relationship with Him. See how Jesus conversed with Him:

"Father, I thank you that you have heard me. I knew that you always hear me, but I said this for the benefit of the people standing here (John 11:41-42)..."

"And now, Father, glorify me in your presence with the glory I had with you before the world began (John 17:5, NIV)..."

"Righteous Father, though the world does not know you, I know you, and they know that you have sent me (John 17:25, NIV)..."

Using Jesus as your righteous guide, do what he did: communicate with God; here's an example:

"Father, I'm going through some tough times right now, but you say that you are my **'refuge and strength in times of trouble** (refer to Psalm 46:1)'..."

"I will be strong in you and your mighty power (refer to Ephesians 6:10) because you give strength to my weariness and you increase my power (refer to Isaiah 40: 29)..."

Also, you can use real life examples to associate what you are trying to communicate to God (reference to Critical Shift 6: Activate Faith...With Your Natural Life):

"Just like a cut on my skin heals itself, I know Lord that you will heal any situation somehow in my life, and I am grateful;"

"As I pay attention for my personal safety when I cross the street for any oncoming traffic, I will be equally careful to maintain my loving contact with you Lord..."

Instead of being distracted by your challenges in life (as The Deceiver cleverly tries to do), turn your challenging issues into an opportunity to re-forge your body, mind, and spirit into a 'full-blown communicator' with God:

"But my God shall supply all your need according to his riches in glory by Christ Jesus (Phil 4:19, KJV)."

"And God is able to make all grace abound toward you; that ye, always having all sufficiency in all things, may abound to every good work (2 Cor. 9:8, KJV)."

Sure, you may not be used to this kind of communicating...

It's not that hard, and you've already done so...for example:

Have you ever loved or truly respected someone in your life? Someone with whom you can trust with your deepest, innermost secrets, and trusting that they will give back as much love and respect for you...probably even more?

If you can do this with someone in the natural world, then you can certainly do the same thing in the spiritual...

Only that you are not left alone in this venture: God's got your back!

Planting Good Mind Seeds...With 'One-Liner Prayers'

Life is a challenge; your time is used to the max, and you are trying to find ways to save some time to do the things that you want...and not just the things that you have to do...

Sometimes, your mind may not be up to communicating with God due to your limited time...

Understand this: God is with you all the time! He is always present in your life, so anything that takes your mind off God is an opportunity for the Enemy to separate you from your personal relationship with Him. It only takes a small situation to start your separation, and if unchecked, then the gap will expand...

"Yeah but I can't be thinking of God all the time!" you might say.

It is true that your mind may be cluttered-up by so many issues, but there is always room to spend some quiet time with The Lord...

Just as you always think of those you love, keep God in mind with simple thoughts and "one-liner prayers." One-liner prayers can pack a powerful spiritual punch, especially if done with intentional Love!

When confronted with your challenges in life, don't avoid your contact with God: take the spiritual offensive (Ch. 20)!

Examples:

a) you have a specific challenge at work that aggravates you: don't start swearing and complaining: use your anger usefully and say: "I know Lord that The Enemy is trying to separate me but I will keep my gaze toward you Lord, and be saved (ref: Isaiah 45:22, NIV)."

b) in your strained relationship...reach into your heartfelt intention, and say: "The Enemy is trying to use my strained relationship to separate me from you Lord, but I will hold onto to your Hand Lord with love and expectation because you are Love my Lord (ref: Colosssians 3:12-14);

c) you need to cut the grass, paint the deck, clean the house, and no time to do it, and are annoyed about it, say: "Lord, I look upon you in with a loving heart to change my anger into useful energy to do my chores..."

You can either use one-liners by referencing verses in the Bible; but what makes God rejoice even more is when using your own heartfelt words to relay good and loving intentions toward Him.

Don't you do the same thing with someone who you absolutely adore?

Who said that your communication with God has to be long-winded, ritualistic, boringly repetitive (even God probably gets bored with ritualistic and repetitive words!)...?

Sometimes in life, few creative words are the best way..!

Simply and lovingly, invite God into your life with humble expectation; it's the same expectation as:

i) when you expect friends over for coffee;
ii) just as you wait for some important news...etc.

Reaching out to God in humble expectation is communicating confidence that He has you covered at all sides:

"A thousand may fall at your side, and ten thousand at your right hand, but it shall not approach you, You will only look on with your eyes, and see the recompense of the wicked (Psalm 91:7,8)...."

As you can see, the "not having time" excuse doesn't work. Don't have the time? Use the one-liners with the intentional expression to stay linked-in to God; speak it out now, with love:

"Feel my life with you in it, my loving Lord;"
"Be with me as I build up all that I do today Lord My Helper;"
"Let's celebrate our relationship, my loving God;"
"I look upon you Lord, and I am awed by you..."

Critical Shift #9: Divided and Conquered...NO MORE!

The Enemy had his conspiracy planned for a very long time:

1) He has clouded your understanding of who you are: a person born to communicate;

2) Mis-aligned you in a position of Ignorance-Laziness Indifference and Forgetfulness;

3) Has imprisoned your life with Temptations, Distractions, and Complications;

4) You struggle spiritually because your thinking has been set off-course and trapped in self-serving, ritualistic, and boringly repetitive acts of religiosity that leads to nowhere...

In other words, The Enemy has separated you from a well-balanced relationship with God and possibly with your world. Satan's entire mission is to divide and conquer. Yes, you can say it's all Satan's fault or God's fault, or life's fault in general...

But this is no time to play the 'blame-game or self-pity...'

You've come to this final critical shift: knowing that Satan's only interest is to cut you off from God in any way possible by creating situations meant to separate (using other religions, other 'feel-good' philosophies, circumstances meant to distract, etc.).

It's time to pick yourself up, and understand that anything that separates you from God needs to be **recognized, exposed and spoken to with the Word by the Reconciler of communications, which is Jesus**.

Even more important: gaze upon the Lord with amazement, with awe, as if you are about to meet your favorite athlete, your favorite movie-star, your hero...you understand the feeling, right?

Want some more help with that?

Well here it is:

Look at the great majesty of your world: the mountains, the trees, the plants...every one of them were created; each cell and DNA was assigned to each to become what they are.

It is no coincidence: everything in this world has been manufactured and assigned a certain formula (examples):

-Rocks have their own formula of existence;
-Plants have their own formula to exist the way they are;
-Water has its own formula;
-Your flesh has its own formula assigned...

You can't blend a rock with flesh...it won't work, and live (aside from science-fiction movies of course LOL!)...certain things can be blended, while others can never be...

And all things that exist are empowered in existence by some kind of mystical energy so that they can exist and not fall apart...the energy came from The Creator:

"Then the Lord God formed a man from the dust of the ground and breathed into his nostrils the breath of life (Gen 2:7, NIV)...

How awesome is that?

Imagine having a personal relationship with someone like that...!

Even more amazing is that God The Creator wants personal contact with you...HIS BREATH IS WITHIN YOU !!

Exciting anticipation, right?

Remember your critical shifts:

1) Your natural life is only the beginning;
2) Your life provides the clues for your contact with God;
3) You are pre-approved to reach out to God;
4) You are welcomed in His House;
5) Trust God as you trust special people in your life (even more);
6) Your good, virtuous intentions can connect to the spiritual;
7) Keep your natural and spiritual self in harmonious balance;
8) Use The Word to overcome any circumstance;
9) The Enemy cannot keep you away from God...

No more waste: you must use your good and noble experiences in life to associate heartfelt communications with the Lord:

You love beautiful sunsets...appreciate the company of your

spouse...have a great friendships...enjoy the company of your kids...enjoying your job...love to play sports...barbeque a steak...your love of nature...you like being nice to others...etc.

Can you dedicate your good emotions and actions to God? Can you invite Him to feel the joy of your reaching out to Him unconditionally?

And don't be afraid to speak with Him every day even if the talk is brief (don't you do the same with your wife, your husband, your kids, your co-workers, your friends, some strangers...?):

-Are you glad? Don't keep it only for yourself: show your gladness to God...speak to Him about it (Example: "Look at me Lord! I am glad and I just want you to see me...thanks for being here with me Lord!) just as a little kid seeks approval from his dad for scoring a at the ball-game...

-You work hard? Be a team-player with God: let Him be involved in your work ("Father, you and I together...we're going to do the best work ever!")...

-You angry? Use the same energy to push aside any distraction from your personal relationship with God (example: Lord, this situation is really getting me mad, but I'm looking toward you Father with great awe my Hero...my anger and the situation that angers me is irrelevant knowing that your Power will help me channel the angry energy for a good and useful purpose...");

-You sad/discouraged? Express your heartfelt desire to be near Him ("I am so discouraged Lord, but I reach out to you my Saviour because your presence in my heart soothes me; I know that you will somehow heal my pain for the better...etc")...

From this day on, you shall channel whatever emotional/physical distraction to useful energy:

- First recognize that a negative situation is meant to separate you from God;
-Use the energy to speak out to the Lord with intention;
-Express your willingness to stay in-touch with Him, and that you want to be together with Him (as a child to his father);
-Gaze upon His Awesomeness and leave the problem to Him...

This is a renewed way of life:

"...forgetting those things which are behind and reaching forward to those things which are ahead, I press toward the goal for the prize of the upward call of God in Christ Jesus (Philippians 3:13-14, NKJV)."

So press forward toward your new goal of freedom in God's Winners' Circle!

Chapter 23

Imagination and Visualization: Your Powerful Communication Channel To God

It has been said long ago by the ancient philosopher Plato that the answers to the universe are already here...you only need to find them!

Every subject known to humankind is here for you to discover and experience, whether it is politics, religion, science, business, sports, language, transportation, engineering, urban-planning, medicine, tools, theater, outer space, video games, raising kids, cooking, personal identity, making friends, handling problems, falling in love, riding a bike, woodworking, communicating...etc.

It usually starts through your Imagination and Visualization.

When the Wright brothers discovered the power of flight, they didn't just assemble their airplane by chance; with the help of nature's wonderfully engineered creatures (in this case birds) the brothers imagined and visualized how their aircraft should be built to sustain flight...And that's only one example; every discovery, every enterprise has undergone some degree of imagining and visualizing before becoming a reality...

Have you ever used your imagination, or visualized some image or concept in your mind?

-starting your own business;
-trying out for the baseball team;
-new ideas for your workplace;
-ideas for redecorating the living room....etc?

You've likely have had creative thoughts millions of times thoughout your lifetime!

Imagination and Visualization are implanted in your nature; they are meant to encourage curiosity, to motivate. It is an inner message to your mind, your soul; it is both instinctive and intentional...it is communication (recall in Ch.1, that you are born to communicate on a verbal, physical, mental, and spiritual level?).

To repeat: **You are all about communication.** Imagination and Visualization are also a form of communication implanted in you; they are signals: a desire in your heart to strive forward and evolve, to understand who you are, to be better, reach higher...

It starts from the moment you were born; imagination and visualization begins early, during your childhood: you begin to play and pretend, and you start imagining and visualizing that:

"I wanna be a fireman," or "I wanna be an astronaut," or "wanna be a nurse..." are some examples you hear kids say.

As innocent as it looks, there is a higher purpose to all this:

imagination and visualization is a natural human development of communication. It will first lead you into natural revelations, and eventually into spiritual ones, unless you get stuck in an 'earthly rut' and have become a victim of Satan's Weapons Of Total Chaos...

Do you realize the unique power that God has given you with this ability called communication? It is more than just talking about practical matters or gossiping; it is an all-encompassing process:

1. imagining and visualizing what you can do;
2. using imagination and visualization to plan physical action;
3. eventually evolve from a physical world, and into the spiritual.

It's all due to your incredible ability of communication: imagination and visualization are also forms of communication, if you use it right!

From Nothing To Something

Jesus said that through faith you can "tell the mountain to get up and be tossed into the sea" (Matthew 17:20). In a way He is telling you, "imagine how far you can reach with your faith!"

Spiritually, you can raise your faith to a level where Satan's Weapons Of Total Chaos become ineffective; simply imagine and visualize yourself reaching out in harmonious contact with God...and let go of Ignorance-Laziness-Indifference-Forgetfulness.

Jesus already said what you have to do:

"...seek, and you will find (Matthew 7:7, NKJV)..."

Easy isn't it? It isn't some kind of secret formula: **seeking and finding is built into your nature,** a natural intention of setting your mind to find the answers to whatever interests you.

Understand the true significance of your own imagination and visualization...and use them to push out, expand, reach higher for the good and noble things in life and beyond: imagine and visualize your relationship with God.

Use Your Natural Life As Reference

It has been already mentioned that your natural and spiritual life must work together in balanced harmony; do not separate the two: God made you both a natural and spiritual person, both complementing each other...

Don't limit your imagination and visualization to your natural life; use this unique communication tool to help you reach out to God!

You've already been using your imagination and visualization plenty of times (examples):

-to renovate your home;
-to start a relationship;
-to plan a business idea;
-to solve an issue;
-to orgnanize a wedding;
-to raise your kids...etc.

You've been using your imagination and visualization hundreds of thousands of times...

In the the previous chapter (Critical Shifts), the second Critical Shift suggests that you extend your experiences in your natural life to help you reach out in the spiritual.

So imagine and visualize yourself:

-sitting on your porch with God;
-walking down the street with Him;
-watching television together;
-at work, by your side;
-in the kitchen as you prepare supper...etc.

"It's impossible to think of Him all the time during my busy schedule!" you might say...

Here's the PROOF THAT YOU CAN DO SO:

-do you think of those you love in the back of your mind during the course of your busy day, if they are doing well?
-are you thinking of your bills in the back of your mind when at home or work, on how much to pay this month to lower the debt?
-have you ever thought about a special event coming up soon in the back of your mind while going through your day (your upcoming vacation, your reservation to the ball game next week, your daughter's wedding six months from now, etc.)?

If you've been thinking about other things in the back of your mind, then you can also think of God being there with you...

Try imagining and visualizing God in everything that you do because:

God is everywhere...The Lord owns the universe!

TEMPTATION-DISTRACTION-COMPLICATION

Of course Satan has other plans for you...making sure that you fall into other kinds of imagination and visualization...distracting ones, influenced by Temptation-Distraction and Complication: imagining and visualizing 'me-first', thirst for power, egotistical pursuits, intolerant, arrogant, selfish...etc, and without God or Jesus in the picture.

Temptations, Distractions, and Complications are working in secret, unseen, shifting your imagination and visualization toward the 'sugar-coating' of earthly life only, steering you off-course and away from the pleasure of relating with God:

"But those who desire to be rich fall into temptation and a snare, and into many foolish and harmful lusts which drown men in destruction and perdition (1 Timothy 6:9, NKJV)."

Getting what you want out of life is fine, and God wants you to have the best...but it isn't fine if you intentionally place God second place (or no place), while your lusts come first:

-Falling for Tempting imaginations and visualizations,
 causing Distractions;
-Complications rising from bad decisions;
-A deepening Ignorance of your incredible importance of
 imagination and visualization;

-In a Lazy state, turning to easy visions of earthly pleasures, ignoring the spiritual;
-Indifferent to visions of the supernatural;
-Forgetting about your true power to harmonize your imagination and visualization with the spiritual...

And then you end up complaining to God...but do you realize that:

"You ask and do not receive, because you ask wrongly, to spend it on your passions (James 4:3, ESV):"

In other words, you are using your gifted powers...poorly.

Sincerity In Your Communications

Ask yourself:

"Can you ever make a good connection with someone if your intentions were not sincere?"

Of course not! The connection would be superficial and fake. As in real life, The Deceiver can twist your imagination and visualization to do you great harm, by aligning your communication-intentions solely on selfish, non-spiritual pursuits...

Understandably, it's a challenge at first to imagine and visualize spiritually, especially with all the earthly pleasures, the pains, the wants, the desires, the passions...it can be truly overwhelming!

Instead of falling into Satan's trap of spiritual disconnection by getting drowned in the visions, anxieties and desires of the natural life, imagine and visualize yourself reaching out to God; do so with a sincerity that is not selfish; show heartfelt and transparent intention to bond with Him by visualizing a lovely relationship with God, totally awed by the majesty of His genius: His awesome creativity of the universe, of your own existence (the engineering of your body, of all things created, etc)...

Imagine and visualize your love and appreciation for Him as you would your favourite personality here on earth: your husband/wife, a movie star, a sports hero, your favorite novelist...etc. Love The Lord with all your heart, unconditionally, sincerely, and show your love for Him by demonstrating that you appreciate the moments in your natural life too:

"Whoever desires to love life and see good days, let him keep his tongue from evil and his lips from speaking deceit (1 Peter 3:10, ESV)..."

Use your imagination and visualization to re-align yourself to a peaceful mindset on earth, and seek the spiritual fellowship with God...

Get close to the Lord...by leaving some room for Him in your heart:

-imagine and visualize God sitting with you on the porch, or:
-walking with Him (your back yard, the park, the street, etc.);
-sitting quietly by the fireplace with the Lord;
-going together at the baseball game;
-watching t.v;
-with your group of friends or family activities;
-At the gym...etc!

Expect God Everywhere And In Everything

God is everywhere; His "signature" is on everything that you see, touch, feel, and think.

Can you imagine it? Visualize it?

He is here right now; His signature is even on you!

God is not reserved just for "prayer-times, " moody and dark moments, and time-schedules that suit you or your religion...

He wants you to share the joy of your life-experience with Him every moment:

-just as you envision the joyous company of your wife;
-as you share your love with your kids;
-enjoying the company of good friends;
-good memories;
-the company of your parents;
-co-workers;
-community...

As you welcome your loved one in your heart, open your heart and welcome God into your life too. Imagine and visualize extending a warm welcome to Him, as you would welcome someone you know...

The Lord expects you to reach out to Him...

"And why should you think He is expecting it?"

Because communication is a two-way process: you give, and you receive; and it's no different with God...

206

For example:

-do you visualize the thought of your spouse being mindful of you
 throughout the day in the back of her mind?
-do you sense the affection from your family?
-expect that your kids love you?
-do you expect your friends to be mindful of you, call you once in a
 while (invite you to supper, see a movie, etc.)...?

Can you imagine and visualize that God is mindful about you? He
always was, or else He would not have given you the power of two-
way communication, right?

It means that HE WANTS YOU TO COMMUNICATE WITH
HIM...reach out to Him because waits for your loving spiritual
reaching-out:

"And behold, I am with you always, to the end of the age
(Matthew 28:20, ESV)."

"Behold, I stand at the door and knock. If anyone hears my
voice and opens the door, I will come in to him and eat with
him, and he with me (Revelation 3:20, ESV)."

"If anyone loves me, he will keep my word, and my Father will
love him, and we will come to him and make our home with
him (John 14:23, ESV)."

You see, your imagination and visualization are essential
communication tools to start a chain of events in your life: either
negative ones (if you use your imagination and visualization badly)
or expecting good things to come in both your physical and spiritual
life!

Otherwise, what good is it to have imagination and visualization if it is only useful in the natural life?

Your life is not a dead-end...

Activate your own imagination and visualization to blast-off into the spiritual realm; imagine and visualize a spiritually intimate relationship with God, with the same passion and intention as you imagine and visualize:

-your dream career;
-your ideal soulmate;
-a trusted friend;
-great relationships,
-the good and noble moments in your life, etc.

Do the same with God, with the help of His Word:

-imagine and visualize being with Him;
-as your ideal Soulmate;
-a Trusted Friend;
-having a great relationship with Him;
-sharing good and noble moments in your life...!

Life Teaches How To Get In Touch With God...Once you Re-Align Your Mindset

Imagine and visualize God with passion. Welcome Him as your first desire once you have understood that He has been waiting to hear from you. And what's more, He wants to do good things for you...if you open your heart to Him!

"But seek first the kingdom of God and His righteousness, and all these things will be added to you (Matthew 6:33, ESV)."

God doesn't want you to worship Him like some religious string-puppet; He wants an active and living personal relationship with you. He wants you to be 'three-dimensional' when in contact with Him..

That's why you were given the power to imagine and visualize: to see His presence in all aspects of your life with your 'inner eyes' of your heart and mind!

The great news is that God knows when your intentions are sincere. If you are having a tough time getting in-touch with your inner-self, then use your imagination and visualize to tuning-into God; let Him know you are trying, and God will help:

"...I believe; help my unbelief (Mark 9:24, ESV)..." and:
"...ask...seek...knock..."(Matthew 7:7)...

Just as you sincerely reach out to your husband, your wife, your children, your parents, your brothers and sisters, your friends...unselfishly, it isn't fake or pretend: it's a real, intentional act of communication! Use it consciously and intentionally for the spiritual too; you will discover some eye-opening revelations as it helps unify your body, your mind, your soul, and spirit...

Remember who you are: you are a free-willed person who was blessed with the free gift communication, including your tools of imagination and visualization!

So rise above the clutter and do what Jesus did...remove the religious-clutter, and simplify your faith in God:

-use your lessons in life to give you understanding of what is good and noble;

-use the Word in Jesus as your guide to God's Winners' Circle;

-use your imagination and visualization as a communications tool to reach out to God who is right there expecting you to arrive;

-reach out with your humble expectation of reviving your life that is built on both the natural and supernatural!

CONCLUSION

Putting It All Together

You are God's masterpiece of two-way communication; your ability spans beyond the limits of instinct: you are rational, multi-directional, creative, passionate...a three-dimensional person who can communicate on a natural and spiritual level!

You are primed to enter God's Winners' Circle!

You have also come to discover and understand that there is a dark and sinister presence that wants to test and ultimately destroy your right to enter God's domain, and will do everything to re-direct your communications away from the Lord...especially away from Satan's sworn enemy: Jesus!

But now The Enemy is exposed: With Satan's Weapons Of Total Chaos, his purpose is crystal clear:

-cut off your communications with God;
-keep you away from "re-connector" Jesus;
-cause chaos in every relationship in your life;
-to sabotage what is good and noble in your life...

So:

Have you paid attention?
Are you starting to reflect?
Have you come to realize what you are up against naturally and spiritually...and how easy it can be to change all that?

In summary, here is what you've found out:

You are born for a good and noble purpose...

God gave you the power of communication, and the freedom to evolve into a natural and spiritual powerhouse...

You are also Satan's target: he wants to stop your contact with God:

-By sabotaging your power of communication;
-Suppressing you with Ignorance-Indifference-Laziness
  Forgetfulness, and supported by:
-Temptations-Distractions and Complications infiltrating your
  God-given good and noble nature, diverting it away from anything
  spiritual;
-Trapping you in an endless cycles of disconnection;
-Rendering your heart and soul overwhelmingly defenseless;
-Keeping you away from Jesus the Reconciler;
-Attacking your faith at every opportunity;
-Disrupting your mindset, your thinking, your communications;
-Discrediting the supernatural power of the Word in the Bible;
-Hiding his true intentions against you;
-Keeping you cut off by preventing any action based on Love.

But there is Great News: the obstacles behind any spiritual blockage have been identified, isolated, and quarantined. Now you can focus with a greater desire to get spiritually closer to God...with a greater understanding and appreciation of the Word in the Bible; restoring (or solidifying) your relationship with Him...with the help and gentle mentoring of the Savior and Undisputed Champion of God's Winners' Circle: Jesus.

Here is what you can restore with the Lord's help:

-Your understanding that you are born to communicate;
-You've been **pre-approved** for contact with God;
-Expect **unexpected blessings** coming your way;
-That God **welcomes contact** from you;
-**Welcoming God** with anticipation and expectation;
-Your reconciliation must be **intentional and heartfelt**;
-Refuse the weak and defensive posture in your faith;
-You can take an inner **spiritual offensive**, reviving your spiritual passion;
-You can reach out to God with **watchful, uncompromising Love**;
-Extending your uncompromising love to others;
-**Include** God in the works that you do (job, sports, hobbies, entertainment, etc);
-Use your good experience and use the same goodness to open your heart to God;
-**Confide with God**: a close, personal, one-on-one communication;
-Open your heart to Him in **total trust**, even if things look bleak;
-**Envision and imagine** your presence with God in all you do...

What does it all mean?

You've been already saved from the start! God already planted the seeds of your salvation with Christ, but you need to seek out, learn through your mistakes, and re-align yourself for the Grace of salvation to envelop you...

In other words: it is your free destiny to let God get closer to you. And now, you know much more about yourself:

You are pre-approved to enter God's Winners' Circle by living (and sharing) your life with genuine, heartfelt love...a passion that you can extend to others, and equally extend to God.

From this day forward, you are an uncontainable, passionate child of the most High God; you will break through the cloudy barriers of Ignorance-Laziness-Indifference and Forgetfulness, and into the infinitely-clear skies of a harmonious natural and supernatural life. You are already saved by the free gift of Jesus, so there is nothing to prove, except your devotion to God and gratitude for His open and welcoming Hand:

"Humble yourselves therefore under the mighty hand of God, that *he may exalt you in due time* (1 Peter 5:6 KJV)..."

This moment begins a new dawn of understanding in you; may God's Word in Jesus Christ empower you to reach out to a close and personal relationship with both Jesus, God, God's Holy Spirit...and a rewarding life of freedom as never before...

Welcome to God's Winners' Circle!

214

ABOUT THE AUTHOR

George's inspiration for this book began nearly forty five years ago when he was just a kid, when he received his first signal from the Lord...

It wasn't his last...George was called, but just like so many folks out there, he didn't pay close attention to it...

He went along with the flow of life: learning, experiencing life as most folks do in his own personal way.

But he sensed that something was missing: there was no spiritual enlightenment; something was not there. In fact, the knowledge he gained only weighed him down and distressed him, leaving him with an unsatiable desire to seek out for something else...he even studied other ideas, philosophies, trends; still, there was a confusing void that no knowledge could fill...

The Lord was still calling, but George's mindset was not there: life, and its challenging reality had taken over, keeping him distant, prioritizing the natural life over the spiritual, and falling into Temptations, Distractions, and Complications of living...

He too became a prodigal son...caught by the pleasures, needs, and temptations of this world, distancing himself from the Lord.

But the Lord never let him go, even if he was a "hard-case"...He intervened in his life and nursed him back on-course to return to Him, and fulfill his long-standing calling: this book, this newly reborn, rewarding life...and that's only the beginning!

www.ingramcontent.com/pod-product-compliance
Lightning Source LLC
Chambersburg PA
CBHW021358090426
42742CB00009B/905